Winning with the

CALLER

FROM HELL

Books by Shaun Belding:

Winning with the Boss from Hell
Winning with the Employee from Hell
Winning with the Customer from Hell
Winning with the Caller from Hell

Winning with the
CALLER
FROM HELL

A SURVIVAL GUIDE
FOR DOING BUSINESS
ON THE TELEPHONE

SHAUN BELDING

ECW PRESS

Published by ECW PRESS
2120 Queen Street East, Suite 200, Toronto, Ontario, Canada M4E 1E2

LIBRARY AND ARCHIVES CANADA CATALOGUING IN PUBLICATION

Belding, Shaun
Winning with the caller from hell : a survival guide for
doing business on the telephone / Shaun Belding.

ISBN-10: 1-55022-695-9
ISBN-13: 978-1-55022-695-9

1. Telephone in business. 2. Telephone etiquette. I. Title.
Winning with the . . . from Hell series.

HF5541.T4B44 2005   651.7´3   C2004-907049-5

Cover and Text Design: Tania Craan
Cover photo: Getty Images
Production and Typesetting: Mary Bowness
Printing: Marc Veilleux Imprimeur

This book is set in Akzidenz Grotesk and Minion.

The publication of *Winning with the Caller from Hell* has been generously supported by the Government of Canada through the Book Publishing Industry Development Program. Canada

DISTRIBUTION
CANADA: Jaguar Book Group, 100 Armstrong Avenue, Georgetown, ON, L7G 5S4
UNITED STATES: Independent Publishers Group, 814 North Franklin Street, Chicago, Illinois 60610

PRINTED AND BOUND IN CANADA

ECW PRESS
ecwpress.com

This book is dedicated to:
Brian, Sue, Doug, Cecile,
and whoever invented those amazing buckets.

Alexander's Tether

It shakes and beeps; it chirps and chimes;
It rules your life and steals your time.
Its unseen tether holds you fast,
Although alone you're still harassed.

And when escape you think you've made,
Vacations, weekends planned and laid,
Its siren call clamps like a fist.
Try as you might, you can't resist

The heroin of faceless sound
Compelling you to put all down
And answer to the devil's peal.
There's no escape, you've made the deal.

Your loss of freedom moaned and cursed,
And unseen speakers at their worst,
You swear to break the tight'ning wire
Connecting you to things so dire.

But when without withdrawal begins,
We twitch until the demon wins,
And Bell's addiction comes full bore;
We take the pain and ask for more.

Shaun Belding, 2005

CONTENTS

INTRODUCTION
SO YOU'RE HEARING VOICES . . .   xi

PART ONE   **HELL'S BELLS**

CHAPTER ONE
MAY I ASK WHO'S CALLING?   3

CHAPTER TWO
FIRST THINGS FIRST: ENVIRONMENT AND
   ETIQUETTE   17

CHAPTER THREE
IT'S NOT WHAT YOU SAY . . .   49

CHAPTER FOUR
ACTUALLY, IT IS WHAT YOU SAY . . .   81

CHAPTER FIVE
THE MOST IMPORTANT COMMUNICATION SKILL
   YOU WILL EVER LEARN   95

CHAPTER SIX
MANAGING YOUR EMOTIONAL STATES   111

PART TWO **A HOPE IN HELL**

CHAPTER SEVEN
LIFT THE RECEIVER 123

CHAPTER EIGHT
LISTEN TO YOUR CALLER 125

CHAPTER NINE
INVOLVE YOURSELF 145

CHAPTER TEN
FOCUS ON THE ISSUES 153

CHAPTER ELEVEN
THANK YOUR CALLER 161

CHAPTER TWELVE
SILENCE IS NOT GOLDEN 165

CHAPTER THIRTEEN
ACCENTS AND LANGUAGE BARRIERS 175

PART THREE **THE HOUNDS OF HELL**

CHAPTER FOURTEEN
CALLS OF THE WILD 183

CONCLUSION
THIS IS YOUR WAKE-UP CALL 203

SO YOU'RE HEARING VOICES . . .

We have developed a true love/hate
relationship with the telephone.

Even though you can't see the face behind the disembodied voice piercing its way through your headset, there's no problem conjuring up a vivid mental image. Beady, nasty little eyes. Sharp, pointy, unbrushed teeth. Knotted, mousy hair. Sunken cheekbones. Jutting chin. Oh, yeah, and horns — you're pretty sure there are horns. The Caller from Hell — Alexander Graham Bell's personal contribution to our workday stress.

I often wonder if Mr. Bell, toiling in his little Boston workshop with his assistant Thomas Watson, knew what he was getting us all into. Could he possibly have envisioned that telephones would number in the billions by the new millennium? In his wildest fantasies, could he have imagined that millions of people would one day walk around with little versions of his creation in their purses and pants pockets? Could he have known that the telephone would quickly cease to be just another invention and become instead a tool that would shape our very culture and the way we interact in our business and personal lives?

As legend has it, Mr. Bell made his first test call in his workshop to Mr. Watson on March 10, 1876, and uttered the now famous words "Mr. Watson, come here, I want you." Perhaps Mr. Bell would have got a glimmer of things to come if — instead of Mr. Watson's enthusiastic "I can hear you! I can hear the words!" — he'd been interrupted with "Please hold, your call is important to us. An operator will be with you shortly. . . ."

We have developed a true love/hate relationship with the telephone. All you have to do is look at the twitchy behavior of a businessperson who has been deprived of his or her cell phone for a few hours to appreciate our dependence on phones. Yet at the same time, there always seem to be undercurrents of resentment toward the raw intrusiveness the telephone represents. There's no polite knock, no inquiry as to your availability or interest — it just rings. And try as we might to ignore its persistent peals, its demands to be answered are virtually irresistible.

When it comes to doing business, the telephone is invaluable. It's part of your connection to the rest of the world, and, while you can love it or hate it, there's really no way to avoid it. It's also an essential part of customers' connection to you. It's part of your face to the public. And the public is not always happy.

Difficult callers — Callers from Hell — contact you for a number of reasons. Some have problems they want you to resolve. Some want something you can't give them. Some just want to vent their frustration or anger. At some level, Callers from Hell are usually customers. They could be external customers, for whom you or your company provides goods or services, or internal customers, those within your company to whom you provide support.

Whoever they are, and whatever the reason they're calling, the benefits of being able to resolve a situation quickly and positively cannot be overstated. An overwhelming body of research tells us that a single conflict with an organization can have far-reaching consequences in long-term customer satisfaction, and that there exists a direct correlation between customer satisfaction and profitability. In *Modeling the Relationships between Process Quality Errors and Overall Service Process Performance* (1995), David Collier identifies that the average customer who experiences a service failure tells nine to 10 people about the experience. That's a scary number for people in the customer service business. But if you're a manager or supervisor to whom unsatisfied calls or complaints get escalated, it gets even scarier. A 1998 study by Tax and Brown suggests that only 5% to 10% of dissatisfied customers actually take the time to complain following a service failure. This means that, by the time you've heard one single complaint, there have already been from 10 to 20 negative incidents, with negative word of mouth having spread to between 90 and 200 people. If your company averages one complaint a week, that represents up to 10,000 people having heard something negative about the company every year. How many complaints do you get a week, a month, a year? You may find the results of doing the math unsettling indeed.

The secret to success for most businesses lies in a company's ability to retain its customers. In fact, a 1990 study by Reichheld and Kenny shows the direct link between satisfaction and profitability, establishing that a five-point improvement in customer retention can lead to an increase in profits from 25% to 80%. Learning how to reduce and resolve conflict, therefore, isn't just one of those warm, fuzzy intangibles — it is essential to the health and growth of any business. And it's not just a matter of being *nicer*. Addressing conflict over the telephone requires a number of unique skills.

I am always a little surprised that, despite our familiarity with the telephone, and the intricate ways in which it is woven into our social fabric, so few people have mastered this marvelous communication tool. But perhaps we've simply grown so accustomed to it that we have begun to take it for granted. The fact is that the telephone can be an immensely powerful tool when used properly. And, of course, like most tools, it can also work against you if you're not careful.

The Role of the Telephone

In the business world, the telephone's role continues to increase in importance. In fact, for many people today, the telephone *is* their business. Call centers, from small teams of technical support representatives to huge rooms filled with operators and customer service representatives (csrs), comprise one of the fastest growing segments in business today. But it's not just call centers where the role of the telephone is surging — it's everywhere. A real estate lawyer friend of mine with a burgeoning practice once confided in me that it had been months since he'd seen a client face to face. The nitty-gritty parts of his communications would go back and forth via e-mail, and when his clients wanted the personal touch that's where the telephone came in. The same holds true for accountants, bankers, brokers. The truth is that — for some of us — if we could phone in a haircut we'd do it.

Doing business over the telephone has tremendous advantages. It's instantaneous, and it's more conducive to accurate expressions of emotion and urgency than its younger but fast-growing sibling, e-mail. It allows us to stay better connected to our customers and provides a handy forum for customer feedback. The downside (there's always a downside) to this wonderful invention is that in some ways it's almost *too* fast, *too* instantaneous.

People can pick up a phone, dial a number, and connect with us in the heat of the moment without first cooling off to think things through. We can use the telephone as a crutch, replacing common sense and basic initiative — speed-dialing a technical support person rather than spending a few moments trying to solve a puzzle on our own. People's unabashed dependence on telephone support has become so widespread, in fact, that many companies have resorted to burying their toll-free technical support numbers in the small print deep within owners' manuals. The hope is that people might eventually give up looking and actually try to resolve things themselves before burdening the tech support group with silly questions.

One of the double-edged swords of the telephone is the lack of the visual component. On the plus side, it gives us a certain amount of anonymity and the ability to create illusion. Let's face it — the whole phone sex business is based on this single benefit of letting imaginations fill in for the visual component. I can't say for certain, but my guess is that the people actually answering the telephones in those services are not the same bikini-clad models showing up on the late-night television infomercials.

The telephone can allow us to be someone we're not or give the appearance of being greater than we are. I remember my surprise at discovering that a salesperson whom I'd been speaking with at what I thought was a large corporate office was actually working out of her trailer somewhere in southern California. Some people are blessed with naturally and wonderfully rich voices that project an image far beyond their physical appearance. (As one call center manager I know with such a voice puts it, "I have the perfect face for a call center.")

The downside of the telephone's audio-only aspect is the profound degree to which it restricts our ability to communicate. Without the benefits of facial expressions, gestures, and body language, we are reliant solely on our voices to carry the burden of expressing emotions, being persuasive, and delivering silent messages about how nice we really are. A great many of the challenges we face on the telephone have to do with this lack of a visual component and the ensuing miscommunications.

I'll never forget monitoring a call to an Internet service provider's technical support representative (TSR). The caller was coming across as cold and uncooperative, speaking in one- and two-word sentences. At one point in the conversation, as the TSR was trying to walk her through a procedure, she interrupted and stated, matter-of-factly, "It's just not working." The TSR responded by saying, "I'm not sure what you mean, ma'am," and was met with stony silence. *She doesn't want this problem fixed, she just wants to make someone feel bad,*

I remember thinking to myself. It was a thought I was soon to become quite ashamed of when an audible sob gave me a clue as to why she hadn't been speaking.

We all know how to use a telephone. It's a pretty simple device to operate. Even in a high-tech, sophisticated call center environment, it doesn't take long to become proficient with the equipment. Like so many skills, though, there is a big difference between being able to use a tool and being able to use it well. I know how to swing a golf club, for example, but, as anyone who has ever golfed with me will attest, I'm a long way from the professional tour. This book is about how to use the telephone more effectively. How to take advantage of its strengths and compensate for its weaknesses. It's about how to deal with difficult situations and difficult callers — those times and people that increase our stress levels and ruin our days. It's about increasing our callers' satisfaction and our enjoyment at work.

Whether you work in a large call center, fielding hundreds of calls a day, or in a small office, dealing with only a handful of calls, the skills outlined here are both relevant and powerful. The telephone is pretty hard to get away from no matter where you live these days, and even the ubiquitous call display can't predict what's in store for you at the other end. It's best to be prepared.

PART ONE

HELL'S BELLS

It seems that you can see, if I hear rightly,
Beforehand whatsoe'er time brings with it.
— DANTE'S *INFERNO*

CHAPTER ONE

MAY I ASK WHO'S CALLING?

We all have limits, and when we reach them it's not unusual for us to begin behaving more than a little out of character.

Jeanne worked in the call center of a mutual fund company during the high-tech meltdown in 2001. As you may expect, she and her coworkers had to deal with more than their share of calls from customers unhappy with the sharp drop in the value of their investments. She was fielding close to 100 calls a day, five days a week, and after a while they all kind of blurred together.

There was one call, however, that stood out. One that Jeanne will never forget. The man was in tears, and his voice reflected both intense anger and deep sadness. He told her of being laid off from his lucrative job in the high-tech sector and how, because of his employment situation, and the dramatic fall in the value of his investments, his life was now in ruins. He was bankrupt, his wife was leaving him, and the bank was taking back his home. When he wasn't weeping, he was shouting at Jeanne, demanding to know how her company could have been so stupid as to not have seen the crash coming.

He talked for over 15 minutes without interruption, and he eventually hung up without giving Jeanne the chance to respond. Just as well, because she was at a complete loss for words. She had recognized the voice — that of her next-door neighbor and longtime friend.

Who are Callers from Hell? All but a small few of them are just regular people like you, me, and Jeanne's neighbor. Most are fundamentally nice, decent people whom you have simply managed to catch at their worst. And it's usually a safe bet that they aren't enjoying the situation any more than you are. So what is making them behave so unpleasantly?

It's a good question. And it's one that we typically don't spend enough time trying to answer. Oh, sure, we ask the question lots of times. "What's his problem?" "Who does she think she is?" "What kind of drugs is he on?" The list goes on. We ask it but rarely try to answer it — which is rather unfortunate because it is the cornerstone to resolving conflict. If I've learned anything over a decade of studying conflict in the work-place, it's that there is almost always more going on with a difficult person than meets the eye. And the better you understand the baggage the person is carrying, the more successful you will be at dealing with conflict.

So let's talk about what's going on in the difficult caller's mind when he's dialing your number. What's motivating him? What's contributing to his emotional state and behavior? There are five fundamental things that contribute to your customers' emotional states and behaviors, five variables that dictate whether they are calling with positive expectations or negative expectations: *needs, personal situation, current circumstances, personality,* and *predisposition.* Let's take a look at each of these variables and the impact that it can have on a caller's behavior.

Needs

Everyone who calls you has a need. She needs to buy something, clarify some information, get some help, or sort something out. It can be a positive need — such as buying a gift for a favorite niece — or a negative need — such as calling to get help for a misbehaving computer. Whether it is positive or negative, when a customer picks up the telephone to make a call, her need is usually at its peak — she has just seen the item advertised on an infomercial, her television just went on the fritz, her credit card has just been declined, she just got your message, and so on. As we discussed earlier, the very nature of the telephone just begs for impulsiveness.

One of the most common errors we make is second-guessing customers' needs. I can't begin to tell you how many situations I've seen in which it was the *serviceperson* who escalated — and at times even created — a conflict with a caller by incorrectly assuming he or she knew why that customer was calling. I remember one such instance in the reservation center of a car rental agency. I was listening to the calls of the call center agents and providing feedback and coaching on how they could improve their closing ratio. While listening to one of the agents, I began to notice a trend. Every customer who called in, of course, began with a question (we'll talk more about this in chapter five), and I'd guess that close to 60% of them started with an inquiry about price, such as "What's your rate for a midsize car?" What was interesting was that the agents had become so conditioned to responding to questions about price that they'd begun to assume that price was the most important issue for *everyone* who called.

One caller, with a very pleasant — positively buoyant — voice, called in to inquire about a car. Here's how the conversation went.

Caller:	Hi! I need a nice car for the weekend. Price isn't important. What kind of full-size cars do you have?
Agent:	We have Monte Carlos, Grand Prix, and Impalas.
Caller:	Hmm. . . . You used to have Cadillacs.
Agent:	Yes, sir, we still have them.
Caller:	Do you have one available for this weekend?
Agent:	Yes, sir. They are quite expensive, though. We do have a

special on midsize cars for $29 a day. Would you like one of those?

Caller: Thanks, but I think I'll take the Cadillac.

Agent: We don't have any specials on the Cadillac this week, sir.

Caller: *[Beginning to get a little annoyed]* I'm not interested in a special. I'm interested in a Cadillac.

Agent: I just want to make sure you get the right car, sir.

Caller: The Cadillac is the right car.

Agent: Yes, sir. It is quite expensive, that's all.

Caller: *[Now becoming angry]* Is there some reason you don't want to rent me a Cadillac?

Agent: *[Sounding irritated]* No, sir. If you want a Cadillac, I'll get you a Cadillac. . . .

It was right about then that the caller hung up. The agent turned to me with a "What was that guy's problem?" look on his face. He had no idea that it was he who had caused the conflict.

The agent lost a high-end rental and frustrated his caller because he completely ignored the caller's needs. The caller wanted a classy car, but the agent assumed he was looking for a deal. Possibly, the agent assumed the caller was like the previous two callers he'd spoken with; perhaps he generally assumed that everyone is looking for a good deal. Whichever the case, he managed to illustrate very effectively why we are always better off not trying to second-guess our callers' needs.

Although this was somewhat an extreme incident, we see people unwittingly making assumptions about other people every day. And every time it happens, you can see the increase in the potential for conflict. Another example is a call I got a while back from a telemarketer trying to interest me in tickets to a circus coming into town in a month. I thought it was a terrific idea but was literally on my way out the door to pick my daughter up. "Sounds interesting," I said, interrupting him. "Can I get you to call back in a couple of hours? I'm just on my way out the door to pick up my daughter."

The telemarketer, assuming that I was yet another customer trying to give him the brush-off, ignored me and began expounding the virtues of the charity that the circus was supporting.

"I really do have to go," I said to him.

"Fine," he said to me disgustedly and hung up.

That was eight months ago, and I'm still waiting for him to call back.

In another instance, I was calling my bank to pass on some nice words about a great experience I'd recently had with one of its CSRs. After navigating through the arduous voice mail system, I finally got a live person and asked to be connected to a supervisor.

"May I ask what it is regarding?" the CSR said coolly.

"I just wanted to pass on an experience I had," I replied.

"Is the problem something I can help with?" she persisted.

"It wasn't a problem — it was a good experience," I said.

"Really?" She sounded surprised.

In both of these instances, the service people wrongly assumed that I had a negative need. You can see how easily such an assumption could offend a customer and create conflict. Never make assumptions about your callers. Each one has a need, which can be either positive or negative, but it's not until you've taken the time to actually listen to the caller that you will know which it is. There is no upside to making assumptions about people.

Personal Situation

Have you ever had "one of those days?" One of those weeks? One of those months? Try as we might to prevent it, our lives are buffeted by outside influences and random occurrences. At any given time, it seems, there is something going on in our lives that is impacting our emotional states. We're getting married or divorced; someone's having a baby or going to a funeral; we're getting a raise or going bankrupt; we're in love or on the warpath. I've always wondered, with all of the daily challenges we face in our own lives, why anyone would feel compelled to watch a reality TV show.

For the most part, we aren't greatly affected by the emotions created from our callers' personal situations. Sure, some callers may come across as a little more pleasant than others, and others may come across as a little more grumpy. But unless you know the person, chances are you won't recognize that his or her behavior is in any way out of the ordinary. And most of us have become fairly adept at keeping our emotions to ourselves. There are extremes, however, and as good as we may be at masking our emotions I think we've all seen how even the nicest of people can begin to behave badly when dealing with a stressful enough personal situation. We all have limits, and when we reach them it's not unusual for us to begin behaving more than a little out of character.

While we rarely have any way of knowing a caller's personal situation, we can sometimes get clues if we pay close enough attention. A caller reluctant to confirm information with a spouse may be having some relationship challenges at home. A caller hesitant to give you a credit card number may be at (or beyond) his limit. When you find yourself mentally asking that question "What is his problem?" there is a good chance that a personal situation is triggering the behavior.

Current Circumstances

Way back in 1990, my wife and I were in the process of losing our business, a small chain of toy stores that had fallen victim to the devastating recession. For a while during this period, I found myself to be a very popular person. The phone at work seemed to be ringing constantly. The only problem was that it was mostly bill collectors on the other end. It wasn't, of course, that I didn't *want* to pay people — I simply couldn't. And the very fact that people were calling me for something I didn't have created a stressful and potentially explosive situation.

The circumstances surrounding telephone contact can be either positive or negative. As anyone who has ever worked in a busy call center can attest, customer "wait time" plays a significant role in the mood of a caller. There's no question that the grouchiness of a caller is directly proportional to the length of time he has to wait and that the grouchiness is compounded by how much of a hurry the caller is in.

A few years ago my company worked with people in the Law Society call center. Their jobs were to advise lawyers on issues of conflict of interest, ethics, and so on. Many times the lawyers were calling from the courthouse — in a recess or just before their case was to be heard — needing an immediate answer to a question for which no quick answer was available. Imagine the challenges in having to deal with time-stressed, high-strung corporate litigators who have been holding in a queue for five minutes. Ew.

The unpleasant circumstances we find ourselves in can have a wide variety of causes — a CSR not having done her job properly in the first place, silly company policies, poor planning, understaffing, et cetera. And these circumstances can happen with even the most well run of companies. Let's face it, computers go down, people get sick — things going wrong are a part of life. The thing about stressful circumstances is that they're typically stressful for both the caller and the service-person. The caller, of course, is allowed to complain about them. Like it or not, we aren't.

Predisposition

I was listening to a radio talk-show host interviewing a teenager about racism in the community. "It's the older people," she said. "Older people are the most likely to make prejudgments about things and other people." She had no idea of the irony of her statement.

The fact is that we all prejudge things. We all have predispositions. Some of us believe that women are more effective salespeople; some believe that men are better team players. Some of us believe that any food served at a fast-food restaurant is unhealthy; some believe that all "health food" is a scam. These predispositions are created by upbringing, education, and past experiences, and they play a significant role in guiding our thoughts and actions.

Unfortunately, when it comes to our callers, many predispositions can work against us. Some callers will assume that you are going to give them a hassle. Some will assume that you don't really care about them. Others will have no faith in your product or technical knowledge. And some people are simply convinced that *everyone* is out to cheat them. On top of everything else, there are many people who, for whatever reason, just plain hate the telephone.

To make things worse, many people with negative predispositions spend inordinate amounts of time preparing for their calls. By the time she dials your number, she's already run through several times in her mind what the call is going to be like. She anticipates the worst, which puts you behind the proverbial eight-ball from the moment you answer the phone.

Many times a caller's predispositions are the result of our own making — with us having created a negative first impression. All too often I hear people expending tremendous efforts to overcome a disastrous first encounter. That old saying "You never have a second chance to make a first impression" couldn't be more true.

Of all the elements that contribute to a customer's perceptions and expectations of us, predisposition is perhaps the most significant and the hardest to change.

Personality

In conducting research for each of the books in my Winning with the . . . from Hell series, I've read over 50 books on conflict resolution, watched dozens of videos, and attended countless seminars. Without question, the most common element in conflict resolution programs is their focus on learning how to read and react to different personality types. This aspect is probably the most significant difference between other approaches to conflict and the approach that I take.

It's not that I don't believe that personalities play a significant role in conflict — they do. It's just that, no matter how good you are, or how much education you have, I don't think you can gauge someone's "personality type" based on an encounter lasting mere minutes — particularly over the telephone. As we've discussed, a lot of other elements contribute to conflict, and everyone — even nice people — can begin to behave in strange ways given the right pressures brought to bear.

Having said this, people's unique personalities are

often the random elements that cause them to behave in otherwise inexplicable ways. Our callers, like all of us, have their own "hot buttons." Triggers that can set them off. And it can be all too easy to unwittingly push someone's buttons, with disastrous results. The secret to avoiding the problems that personalities can create is to pay close attention to how people respond to you and, when you find yourself pushing a button, to make a mental note not to push it again.

Part of the challenge of dealing with different personalities is the difficulty in being objective. Most of us have been guilty at some time or other of assuming that other people are, or should be, like us — that we share the same likes, dislikes, and motivational drivers. Nothing, of course, could be further from the truth, and failure to respect the diversity of personalities and motivations can create huge difficulties in predicting or understanding the behavior of others.

Needs, personal situations, current circumstances, predispositions, and personalities. Five pieces of baggage that every caller carries into Caller from Hell Central. We have little control over these elements, yet they dramatically impact our interactions with callers. Is it any wonder, with all of this going on in a caller's mind, that we so often find ourselves shaking our heads at their behavior?

It is crucial to keep in mind these dynamics of customer expectations if we hope to resolve conflicts with callers effectively. The better we understand these five elements, the better we understand our callers, the easier it becomes for us to manage our own emotional states, and the more effectively we can resolve conflict.

CHAPTER TWO

FIRST THINGS FIRST: ENVIRONMENT AND ETIQUETTE

*If you ever get caught interrupting a caller,
find a big stick somewhere and whack
yourself upside the head with it.*

Have you ever been a Caller from Hell? I have. I don't behave badly often, and I certainly don't think that I ever set out to be grouchy, but on rare occasions it just seems to happen. I don't feel nearly as guilty about it as I used to, though. In my work with call centers, I've probably listened to 500 calls from "Difficult Callers," and at least half of the callers have been the same as me. They start off pleasantly and with good intentions, but then something just seems to push their nasty buttons.

My experience is that most calls from Callers from Hell tend to start off civilly. These callers, despite having negative needs, situations, circumstances, predispositions, or personalities, seem to be willing — at least initially — to give us a chance. But something happens. Something knocks them off the rails of civility and sends the whole call sideways. What goes wrong?

Unfortunately, many times the real culprit is us. Many callers turn into Callers from Hell in reaction to *our* behavior, our companies, and our policies. This unfortunate fact was supported in a 1990 research study, *The Service Encounter: Diagnosing Favorable and Unfavorable Incidents* (Bitner et al.), which demonstrated clearly that it is most often the *employee's response* to negative incidents, not the incidents themselves, that leads to dissatisfaction.

What this suggests is that, while learning how to deal with Callers from Hell is critical to both your business and your emotional well-being, there's a lot to be gained by working on ways to *reduce* difficult calls in the first place — by trying not to shoot ourselves in our collective feet so often. There are a lot of things we have control over that contribute to customer satisfaction and can thereby help to reduce conflict: from adherence to some basic telephone etiquette to making more substantial structural and environmental changes. I've identified what I believe to be the 18 most important things that you and your company can control to maximize customer satisfaction. Work on the ones you can control, and encourage other people to work on the ones over which you have no control.

1. Control Your Environment

Our ability to provide a positive, world-class experience to our customers is dependent to a large extent on our emotional state — on our mood. In addition to the emotions triggered by our callers' behaviors (see chapter six), our moods and corresponding actions are greatly influenced by our surroundings. An overwhelming amount of research points to a wide variety of environmental factors that contribute to our general well-being — colors, open spaces, lighting, et cetera. One study by Texas A&M University, for example, showed that people demonstrate significantly more innovative thinking and generate more ideas and original solutions in offices that have flowers and plants. If you're like most people, you know what it's like to walk into an environment and feel your mood shift.

Unfortunately, though, when working on the telephone, we don't get the same kind of relevant stimulation that people get in other occupations. The retail salesperson is surrounded by product and has customers right in front of her where she can read their body language. The service representative can *see* the broken part and the visibly distressed customer. The HR manager can walk into other people's offices and see the personal mementos, photos, and pictures on the wall. If you conduct most of your business on the telephone, you're in somewhat of a void, and your mind has to fill in a lot of gaps. It helps when you can create an environment around you that puts you in the right frame of mind for doing your job. Learning how to manipulate visual and auditory stimulation is a wonderful way to help you build a productive environment.

I remember working with one particular call center that was trying to improve the effectiveness of its employees. The 40 agents who worked in the center were responsible primarily for collecting money from people who were behind in their payments. It is a difficult and generally unrewarding task and requires a delicate balance between firmness and compassion. The goal, generally speaking, is to try to collect the money from customers without alienating them. The company wanted its money but didn't want to lose customers. As with most call centers of this type, there were two extremes when it came to the agents. Some were a little too aggressive in their efforts, and some weren't quite aggressive enough. We had to try to help both types of agents find the middle ground — we needed to get the aggressive agent to become a little more compassionate and the overly compassionate agent to be a little less focused on the caller's needs and more focused on the company's needs.

We began with an environmental approach. We filled the cubicles of the too aggressive agents with sad pictures cut out from magazines and downloaded from the Internet — images of poverty, hungry children, survivors of disasters, et cetera. The idea was that, when they worked with customers, they'd get a sense of what life can be like for people facing difficult times. For the other agents, we picked visual stimuli of people who were taking advantage of others — images of people being deceitful or self-serving.

The results with both groups were instant and dramatic. By the end of the first week, the overly aggressive employees had reduced the number of complaints about them by more than half — with no reduction in their collection ratio. The other group, the overly compassionate agents, increased their collection ratio by over 25%.

There are various ways to use visual stimuli to impact effectiveness.

In another company we worked with, several salespeople always seemed to be falling just short of meeting their quotas and having a hard time doing those little extra things we knew they had to do to close sales. One of the steps we took was to paper their offices in pictures of tropical islands — so that everywhere they looked they were reminded of why they wanted to close sales more effectively. In one technical support group, our goal was to try to help the techies have more patience with people, not move too quickly, and not use so much technical lingo. So we covered their offices in pictures of little old ladies, frazzled people, young children, and so on.

Don't underestimate the impacts that external stimuli have on your mood. Images, colors, sounds, and even geometrical shapes play a significant role on our emotional states. The growing mountain of research (e.g., Wexner 1954; Schaie 1961, 1962; Kreitler and Kreitler 1972; Adams and Osgood 1973; Byrnes 1983) keeps reinforcing how much control we actually have. All you have to do is create the environment that suits the need. Don't have control over the paint or lighting in your office? Then use posters with specific colors to trigger emotions. Which colors, shapes, or sounds should you choose? The following are various frames of mind and the stimuli that the research suggests will achieve them.

Agreeable

Colors: blue, blue-green, green, red-purple, purple, purple-blue

Shapes: gently curving or relatively straight lines

Sounds: New Age

Happy and positive

Colors: blue, green, pink

Shapes: curves – no sharp angles; lines should move upward
           from left to right

Sounds: not too loud, higher pitches, fast rhythm

Able to concentrate

Colors: blue

Shapes: soft, abstract

Sounds: Mozart

Strong, action oriented

Colors: red

Shapes: straight lines, moving upward from left to right

Sounds: rhythmic, low tones, subdued

Energetic, enthusiastic

Colors: orange, strong red

Shapes: contrasting

Sounds: loud, strong rhythm

Calm, relaxed, poised – prepared for action

Colors: light pink, soft green

Shapes: lines gently sloping from lower left to upper right

Sounds: silence

Winding down

Colors: baby blue, purple-blue, yellow-red

Shapes: irregular, wavy lines

Sounds: light piano, New Age

Sad, unhappy

Colors: black

Shapes: lines sloping from upper left to lower right

Sounds: soft violin

Angry

Colors: flat black

Shapes: irregular, sharp-angled, and jagged lines

Sounds: loud, pounding (grunge, rap)

Unpleasant, edgy

Colors: yellow, green-yellow

Shapes: tight geometric patterns

Sounds: discordant

Have you ever noticed yourself feeling as though you're in a rut? Unmotivated? Having a hard time staying focused? Sometimes the solution can be as simple as a can of paint and a little background music.

2. Reduce Wait Time

Two of the critical metrics that call centers keep their eyes on are "wait time" and "dropped calls." Wait time is the measurement of how much time passes from the moment the customer gets the message "Please hold" to the time she actually gets to talk to a live person. Dropped calls, sometimes called "call abandonment," are the number or percentage of people who finally admit defeat and hang up. As you might expect, there is a direct correlation between wait time and dropped calls, and companies that track these things are soon able to determine the critical threshold. The wait-time threshold is the point at which people are most likely to hang up.

Unfortunately, there is no one magic number — no single acceptable wait time that we can use as a standard. It varies dramatically based on the industry and the reason the customer is calling. The wait-time threshold for a customer impulsively calling a 1-800 line for something he saw on an infomercial can be less than

30 seconds. Someone trying to book an airline ticket or get technical support for a malfunctioning computer, however, may be willing to wait over 30 minutes. The experience of virtually every call center professional I've spoken with, though, is that customer grouchiness increases with wait time and how close he is getting to the threshold. And after someone hangs up, if he actually calls back, his patience level is even less, and his grouchiness factor is even greater.

The one wonderful thing about wait times and call abandonment is the measurability, the direct correlation to profitability, and the ease with which they can be fixed. Once you begin measuring wait time and call abandonment, you can begin putting clear costs to them and decide at which point the cost of lost customers outweighs the cost of increased training or staffing levels. In addition to the immediate costs, you can factor in the long-term impacts on customer loyalty. As wait time increases, call abandonment increases. As call abandonment increases, sales decrease, short-term customer satisfaction decreases, and long-term customer loyalty decreases. The remedy is simple. Increase the number of CSRs to reduce wait time and increase the skills of the CSRs to enhance the quality of the experience for the customer.

3. Apologize for Delays

When you know that your customer has had to wait for an extended period of time, whether in a call queue or on hold, make a point of apologizing for the delay. As we'll discover through the rest of the book, people will forgive a multitude of sins if you can convey the message that you genuinely care about them.

How long is too long? It's a difficult question to answer, but it's always better to err on the side of caution. As a rule of thumb, you should acknowledge any wait longer than 20 seconds. (We'll discuss the customers' concept of time in more detail in chapter twelve). The way in which you express your apology is also important. A mumbled "Sorry" isn't good enough. Neither is a matter-of-fact "I'm sorry it took so long." For the apology to have an impact, your customer has to believe that you mean it.

4. Never Use a Speaker Phone

Speaker phones are wonderful inventions. It's unfortunate that so many people abuse them. Here's the rule of speaker phones: unless you have someone else in your office who is an integral, active part of the conversation, you should never use a speaker phone. Not only is the sound quality poor, but also the message you send to your caller is that she is an interruption — that you are occupied with other things. It can also make people uncomfortable, wondering who might be in the office with you.

5. Have One Conversation at a Time

Have you ever been in the middle of a telephone conversation in which the other person is having simultaneous conversations with others in his office? You're never quite sure which comments are directed to you or how much attention he's really paying to what you're saying. It's kind of like those annoying people with the hands-free cell phones in animated discussions with invisible people in grocery stores or like those store employees wearing the equally annoying headsets. Is the clerk talking to you or the other guy?

I have a client who is notorious for this. I'll be talking merrily away on the phone, and he'll interrupt with "Hang on" and begin to have another, totally unrelated, conversation with someone in his office. This might happen two or three times in a single conversation. I've told him more than once that, if he wasn't such a valuable client, I'd never talk to him on the telephone again. He thinks I'm kidding.

Unless other people are an important part of the conversation (in which case you may want to use a speaker phone), don't split your attention. Dividing your time is a surefire way to irritate people.

6. Ask for Permission to Put Someone on Hold

Whenever you have to put someone on hold, or leave the caller for any reason, make sure you ask permission and explain why you're doing it. For example, "Mr. Moralis, would you mind if I put you on hold for two minutes? I just want to clarify something with my supervisor." Most customers, when they understand why you are doing it, will agree. The waiting becomes much more tolerable when callers understand what they are waiting for.

7. Stay with Your Caller

Whenever you have to transfer a caller to a different person or department, make sure that you cover the bases. Give your caller the proper extension number of the person you are transferring him to just in case the call gets dropped. This way the caller can call back directly without having to revisit hoops that he's already jumped through. It also doesn't hurt to give your caller your extension or direct line, just in case he feels the need to speak with a familiar voice. Finally, while you're transferring a call, try to stay with your caller to introduce him to the next person. This reinforces to the caller that he's important and not just being randomly bounced around the system.

8. Smile

In every customer contact job, people are told about the importance of smiling. It's the one facial expression that can't be misunderstood, and there is no faster way to create a positive relationship. So is smiling important when you're using the telephone? No one, after all, can see your facial expressions, so does it really matter? The answer is an unequivocal yes! As odd as it may sound, a smile can be heard almost as easily as it can be seen.

As we'll discuss in the next chapter, tone of voice has a dramatic impact on how our customers perceive us. A wonderful illustration of this was a dramatic 2002 Harvard study that directly linked the tone of voice employed by a surgeon with the likelihood of that surgeon facing a malpractice suit. But don't rely on other people's research — do a little yourself. The next time you're talking with someone on the phone, try to imagine her facial expressions. Chances are your guesses will be pretty close.

So what can you do to remind yourself to smile? In our call center customer service training programs, we give every participant a mirror to take back to work. All it takes is an occasional glance in the mirror to remind people to make the conscious effort to smile.

9. Identify Yourself

There are hundreds of ways to answer the telephone. Some companies have a specific protocol for how to answer the phone, but they are, unfortunately, few and far between. One of the absolute musts when it comes to call-answering protocol is to ensure that you identify yourself right away. It can be the more scripted, branded approach "Good morning! Thank you for calling Acme. This is Darlene speaking — how may I help you?" or the more professional "Darlene Smith. How may I help you?" Whichever approach you take, your caller is now talking to a person, not just some random voice on the other end of the telephone. Part of the process of building positive caller experience and customer loyalty is creating a connection with that person. And the first step in creating a connection is to give your caller the sense that she is talking to a real person.

10. Use Callers' Names

Another critical part in building that all-important connection to your caller is to use her name. This is, in fact, not just an important rule of thumb with callers but also critical for establishing a connection with anyone. Most people like hearing their names used. It gives us all a sense of importance. And the more often you can use somebody's name in a conversation, the better. If you're with a company in a customer service or technical support role, and the other person's name and information have popped up on the screen in front of you, then use that name.

I remember calling a credit card company with an inquiry about my card. I had dutifully navigated the voice mail system and punched my card number in the telephone keypad, and I was patiently waiting for a customer service representative. Sure enough, 15 seconds later a live person came on the line. But to my surprise — instead of the expected "Good morning, thank you for calling Visa, how may I help you?" — I got a cheerful "Good morning, Mr. Belding! Thank you for calling Visa. This is Joanne, how may I help you?" I was a little startled at first, but the more I thought about it the more I realized that I liked the technique. It made me feel like a somebody — not just another of the hundreds of nameless cardholders Joanne would be speaking to that day.

It got me thinking about all the times I'd called through to somebody's office and my call had been screened by an assistant. And even though the assistant would tell my contact who was on the line, the contact would often answer with just "Hello" — as if he or she didn't know who was on the other end. I made a promise to myself from that moment on that whenever I knew who was on the other end of the ringing telephone — whether she had been prescreened by my assistant or her information had popped up on my call display, I would use her name right away. So now when I hear "Shaun — Jane Smith is on line two," I no longer just pick up the phone and say, "Good afternoon, Shaun Belding speaking," and wait for the response from the person I know. I now pick up the phone and say, "Hi, Jane, how are you!" It's a great way to set the mood right off the bat.

You should really try to use someone's name throughout a conversation — at least two or three times if possible — from the opening "Good afternoon, Mr. Anderson, how may I help you?" to appropriate moments within the conversation. So, for example, instead of saying, "You're absolutely right, you do have a credit of $500 on this account," say, "You're absolutely right, Mr. Anderson, you do have a credit of $500 on this account." In doing so, you make your customer feel closer to your company and to you. He will feel less like just a random caller and more like an important person.

Using people's names, however, can backfire on you if you don't do it properly. Here are some very important etiquette issues to keep in mind.

1. Always Use the Caller's Last Name

Unless it is someone you know very well, or are on an established first-name basis, using a caller's first name is almost always inappropriate. If the person specifically requests that you refer to him or her by first name, then by all means do so. But until that time, it's Mr. or Ms.

It's a different story, however, when you're referring to yourself. When you introduce yourself, you should almost always use your *first* name. The reason for this has to do with fundamental social etiquette. By using your caller's last name and your first name, you are acknowledging that your caller is more important than you are. This is a very important message to convey — both in building relationships with callers and in dealing with callers who are unsatisfied.

2. Use Ms.

Closely related to the first piece of etiquette is how do you refer to a woman on the telephone? Is it Mrs., Miss, or Ms.? Unless otherwise requested by your caller, use Ms.

It's the safest, most appropriate, and least presumptuous honorific.

3. Confirm Pronunciation

The third and most important etiquette issue when using names is to make sure that you confirm how the caller's name is pronounced. Even if it looks slam-dunk simple, it doesn't hurt to ask — because, while using someone's name is a great way to build a connection, mispronouncing that name is a surefire way of driving a permanent wedge between you and your caller. So when you answer the phone with "Good morning, Ms. Smith, this is Jason speaking," just follow up with a simple "Did I pronounce your name correctly?" If your customer does correct you (i.e., "It's Smythe"), it's critical that you don't make the same mispronunciation again. And don't forget to apologize: "Smythe? Oh, I'm terribly sorry. I'm glad I asked!"

If the person's name doesn't automatically pop up on the screen in front of you, and it looks as if you're going to be having an extended conversation (e.g., walking somebody through a lengthy or detailed procedure), it's a good idea to ask. When she gives it to you, write it down so you don't forget it and quickly re-greet her and reintroduce yourself. Here's an example:

> **Caller:**   I'm trying to reinstall this software, and I'm having some challenges.

CSR: Glad to help! Oh, I'm sorry, I didn't catch your name. . . .

Caller: Jane Smith.

CSR: Hi, Ms. Smith, I'm Shaun. Now, what seems to be the problem?

This approach lets your customer know that you are interested in her, and it gives the two of you a more solid connection for your interaction.

11. Remain Professional

A couple of years ago I was investigating having my company participate in a large conference for HR managers. I called the conference company to find out the details of sponsorship, renting booth space, and so on. The sales rep I spoke with started out wonderfully. He was helpful and knowledgeable, and I was encouraged that this might be a good investment. The bubble burst, however, as he began to stray from his presentation. "We guarantee satisfaction," he said. "Well," he continued, "unless it's my ex-wife — nothing would satisfy her. You know what I mean, buddy?" He then went on to make a few more remarks about his ex-wife — an obvious sore spot for him. I couldn't get off the phone fast enough.

In another instance, I was speaking with a CSR for the telephone company one Valentine's Day about some challenges we were having with our account. She, too, did a wonderful job — right up to the end. I finished the conversation by saying, "I hope you have a great Valentine's Day!" She responded with "Oh, that's not likely — I have no one to share it with...." Too much information.

Think of picking up a ringing telephone as lifting the curtain in a play. As soon as the word *hello* forms on your lips, the play has begun, and you are on stage. Your role, your character, is service provider (or technician, or bill collector, or receptionist, etc.). And just as you wouldn't expect an actor to step out of character in the middle of a play, your customers don't want you to step out of character on the telephone. The second you step out of your role you're like Mickey Mouse getting caught ducking around a corner in Disney World to have a cigarette and a swig of whiskey. It's just something that should never happen (and, by the way, never does at Disney World!). The key is to understand your character and to play it to the best of your ability. Leave your personal issues and opinions at home.

12. Avoid Buzzwords

Every industry has its unique buzzwords. Some have more than others, and in some cases, such as the U.S. military, the large number of buzzwords people use almost makes it seem as though they're speaking a completely different language. There are basically three types of buzzwords: jargon — words with meanings co-opted for specific uses; acronyms — new words created out of initials or abbreviations; and tech-talk — language to describe specific technology.

Jargon seems to exist in every environment. Words and phrases such as "win-win," "competency bandwidth," "bio-break," "gap analysis," "core competency," and "cluster teams" are just a few that have hit the business world over the years. Teachers no longer practice the art or science of teaching — they are in "pedagogy." Trainers are no longer trainers — they are "learning facilitators." I was talking once with a CSR about a refund on something that wasn't working quite right, and she said, "Not a problem, I'll just 404 it" — "404" was obviously an internal term the company used for a specific kind of refund. My evil sarcastic side snuck out briefly as I said, "Why don't you just 202 it twice — wouldn't that do the same thing?"

For acronyms, there is no organization more famous than the U.S. military. They must number in the thousands. Here are a few:

SECDEF: Secretary of Defense (not to be confused with SECNAV – Secretary of the Navy – or SECNAVINST – Secretary of Navy Instruction)

MAID/MILES: Magnetic Anti-Intrusion Detector/Magnetic Intrusion Line Sensor

FACSFAT: Fleet Area Control and Surveillance Facility

JINTACCS: Joint Interoperability of Tactical Command and Control Systems

The U.S. military has so many acronyms that it even has to reuse some, such as BDO, which could be Battle Dress Overgarment, Basic Delivery Order, or Blanket Delivery Order, and JAWS, which could be Jamming and Warning System, Joint Attack Weapon Systems, or Joint Advanced Weapon Systems.

And we wonder where the miscommunication comes in.

The best examples of tech-talk can be found in computer technical support centers and automotive service centers. I used to think I felt the stupidest whenever I had to talk to a technical support representative about a misbehaving computer. That is, until my mechanic began to explain the things that were wrong with my car. After 10 minutes of hearing about toe-control links, center differentials, torque steer, aspect ratios, and feedback fuel-air-ratio controls, I began to get a headache. I thought that at any moment he was going to tell me he wanted to reinitialize the warp core and route power to the antimatter inertial dampeners. Beam me up, Scottie.

When you're talking with your caller, try to avoid buzzwords at all times. Most people don't really understand them, they can cause colossal miscommunication, and they can make your caller feel stupid. If there is specific language that you must use, such as "defrag" or "combustion chamber," acknowledge to your caller that it's okay for him not to know the terms, and make sure that you take a moment to explain what you are talking about. For example, "Okay, Mr. Jones, what we're going to do is reconfigure your browser. What I mean by that is that we're going to make Internet Explorer — that's what you use to get on the Internet — do the things we want it to do instead of the things it wants to do. It will take about four minutes, and I'll walk you through it step by step. It's actually pretty straightforward, but if I use a term you're unfamiliar with please just let me know. . . ."

One of the best ways to put a caller at ease is to *give her permission* to be confused. Acknowledge that you are using generally unfamiliar terms and that it is easy to become confused. This approach makes it easier for your customers to ask questions without feeling stupid. And don't make the mistake of thinking that, by using buzzwords, you will be perceived as more intelligent. Chances are your caller will think of you only as more unlikable.

13. Don't Interrupt

One guaranteed way to irritate someone is to interrupt her. And if you really want to get under her skin, interrupt her frequently. Interrupting is a symptom of not listening, and if you ever get caught at it (e.g., when a customer says, "You keep interrupting me!") find a big stick somewhere and whack yourself upside the head with it. Listening, as we'll discuss in chapter eight, is the most critical aspect of defusing and winning with difficult situations.

One of the biggest traps that we fall into is when the customer begins describing something you've heard a hundred times before. To save time (and to save having to hear it for the 101st time), you interrupt your customer to move toward the solution. Unfortunately, while you may have heard the problem a hundred times before, it's the first time for your customer. And when you don't appear to be listening to what she's saying, she might assume that you don't fully understand the situation and consequently won't have confidence in your response. The other danger in this trap is that, because you aren't bothering to listen to the end, you could miss some critical information that can help you to find a more efficient solution.

Interrupting is hard behavior to correct because most of us don't realize when we're doing it. When I'm coaching people who habitually interrupt callers, I implement the two-second rule. They have to wait for two full seconds of silence before they may begin speaking at any time. (I get them to count steamboats — "One steamboat, two steamboats" — just like when we used to play hide-and-go-seek.) Most are surprised at how much more their customers have to say. Interrupting people is a fundamental etiquette no-no, and there are very few circumstances in which it is acceptable.

14. Lose the Food, Drink, and Gum

It's amazing all the little sounds that a telephone can pick up. And it's amazing how thoroughly disgusting chewing, slurping, gulping, and swallowing sound over the telephone. Never, ever eat, drink, or chew gum when you're doing business on the telephone. (Or doing business in person, for that matter.)

15. End on a Positive Note

The way you end a telephone call is almost as important as how you start it. There are two things you want to convey at the end of each call:

1. that you enjoyed/appreciated speaking with the caller; and

2. that you wish the caller well and/or look forward to talking with him or her again.

The etiquette of ending a call is simple yet not nearly as common as it should be. Here are some examples:

- Thanks for calling, Mr. Demers, have a great weekend!
- It was great talking with you, Ms. Hooper. Take care!
- Thank you for your business, Mr. Little. Have a great day!
- This was fun — you should call more often! Talk with you soon.

The graciousness with which you end a call plays a big role in how your caller will remember you.

16. Hang Up Last

Sometimes, if we hang up a little too early, and the caller hears the click of the receiver, he can get the impression that he's just been brushed off. Sometimes, too, he may have some additional questions, which he now can't ask. To ensure that your caller feels as though you are with him right to the end, at the conclusion of a call let the caller hang up first.

17. Be Cheerful

The giant property development company Hammerson used to have a receptionist who was, without question, the most cheerful person I have ever spoken with on the telephone. With three words — "Good morning, Hammerson!" — you knew you'd just called the happiest company ever. She sounded like Mary Poppins on steroids, and I loved her. I used to joke that I would call her every morning just to get me motivated for the day.

Cheerfulness is contagious. Just try to stand around a really cheerful person without finding yourself smiling after a while. Even the most crusty of us are eventually won over. My friend Mark Weisleder, lawyer and author of *Real Estate Agents* BEWARE, loves to lightheartedly tell audiences how much he hates people who are happy all the time. "They're annoying!" he'll decry. "Nobody is that happy. I just want to shake them and say, 'Be normal for once — be grouchy!'" Despite his protestations, however, Mark will be the first to tell you that, like the rest of us, he prefers to be around people who make him smile.

"Yabut," people often say to me (I always get yabuts when it comes to being cheerful), "nobody is happy all the time, and it will turn callers off if they think I'm being insincere. Are you suggesting that I be a fake?" No, I'm not suggesting being fake; I'm suggesting being professional (see point nine above). The second you pick up the telephone, you're on stage and in character. Your moods and personal problems are irrelevant to your callers and have no place in your role. Besides, I suspect that most callers, given the choice, would far prefer false cheerfulness over sincere grumpiness any day. Even Mark.

18. Be Positive

I've left the most important point to the last. The one element that must be present whenever someone calls is a positive attitude. Having and projecting a positive attitude is the best way to maximize your odds of having positive interactions with customers and minimizing their dissatisfaction. People are remarkably forgiving when the person on the other end of the phone is positive and cheerful. And, not coincidentally, positive people seem to get a lot fewer Callers from Hell.

What is the difference between positive and cheerful? Cheerfulness is one way in which a positive attitude is expressed. Cheerfulness stems from a positive attitude. Acting cheerfully without having a positive attitude underneath it is where, as mentioned above, you run the risk of being insincere. It always helps when your behavior is a genuine expression of your attitude.

But can you really control your attitude, or is your attitude primarily dependent on outside influences? The answer is that you can absolutely control it! As we discussed above, physical environment plays a significant role in mood. And there are many other ways to influence our attitudes once we've made the choice to change them. *The key word here is choice.*

Learning how to control your attitude starts and ends with choices. You have to *choose* to have a good attitude. You have to *choose* to look at the positive aspects of the world around you instead of the negative aspects. You have to *choose* to be happier. Once you've made a commitment to changing your attitude, the rest will fall into place.

Making any change in your life is, of course, never easy. And when it comes to attitude, we have a number of things working against us. For starters, a lot of our negative outlooks on life have been with us for a great many years, and our patterns of thought are deeply ingrained. To make changes in those deeply ingrained attitudes, you have to be truly motivated to make changes.

One other challenge in trying to change attitudes is that, to admit you want to improve your attitude, you first have to accept you have control over your attitude. And for you to believe you have that kind of control, you have to abandon any semblance of a "victim mentality." By this I'm referring to the temptation to blame everything on someone else. "My parents made me the way I am." "My boss is undermining my career." "My coworkers make me grouchy." And so on.

Unfortunately, some of us really *enjoy* having a victim mentality. And the truth is there's a lot of freedom that comes when you don't have to take the blame for anything. After all, when you're the victim, you don't have to accept any responsibility. And when you're the victim, you always have an excuse for things not going your way. Everything is everyone else's fault. Yes, excuses are wonderful things.

Make the choice to have a positive attitude. It's the best way to effectively minimize the number of unsatisfied customers with whom you have to interact.

Here again are the 18 most important things that you and your company can control to maximize customer satisfaction.

1. Control your environment.
2. Reduce wait time.
3. Apologize for delays.
4. Never use a speaker phone.
5. Have one conversation at a time.
6. Ask for permission to put your caller on hold.
7. Stay with your caller.
8. Smile.
9. Identify yourself.

10. Use callers' names.

11. Remain professional.

12. Avoid buzzwords.

13. Don't interrupt.

14. Lose the food, drink, and gum.

15. End on a positive note.

16. Hang up last.

17. Be cheerful.

18. Be positive.

CHAPTER THREE

IT'S NOT WHAT YOU SAY . . .

If there is a common denominator with
every difficult caller we get – that every irate, nasty,
misbehaving caller has in common – it's that
he or she believes we don't care.

Most of us, at a very early age, learned the old maxim
"It's not what you say but how you say it." And I suspect
that most of us have seen more than one example when
people have said the right things in the wrong ways, with
unfortunate results. Our ability to influence people is
very much dependent on our ability to manage tone of
voice. And make no mistake — whether our callers are
looking for customer service, technical support, information, or just someone to listen to, at some level we are
trying to influence them. We want to influence how they
perceive us and how they perceive our company. We
want to influence their moods and understanding. We
want to influence their buying patterns, their satisfaction, and their loyalty. And with Callers from Hell, we
are trying to persuade them that we're not the enemy.

Your ability to influence other people is dependent
on your command of five elements — what I refer to as

the Five Cs of Influence. They include *comprehension, compassion, competence, confidence,* and *cheerfulness.* Let's take a look at each.

Comprehension

Several years ago my computer decided to quit on me at an exceedingly inopportune time. I was 600 miles from home, and it was the day before I was to present a large new-business proposal. The proposal was in the form of a PowerPoint presentation that, of course, was buried in my dead computer. After much frantic searching for the computer company's technical support line (I had it stored in my computer, but . . .), I was finally able to reach a technical service representative. I explained my situation and how important it was for me to, at the very least, retrieve my presentation.

I managed to control my panic as the technical rep took me through a long series of diagnostic procedures. After much deliberation and many hmmms later, he came up with his solution. He began with "Okay, Mr. Belding, here's what yergunnahafta do. Package your computer up and send it to . . ."

My frustration level, needless to say, jumped a few notches when it became clear to me that he simply didn't understand what my *real* problem was. Whether I got my computer repaired at that moment was far less relevant to me than simply retrieving my PowerPoint presentation. I think my frustration with both the TSR and the situation weren't as well masked as I would have liked them to be, and in the ensuing but brief conversation I suspect that I climbed up a few notches on this guy's Caller-from-Hell-o-Meter.

I eventually hung up and called right back, hoping that I would get someone else. I did, and the new TSR handled the situation much better. And even though he, too, was unable to resolve the situation, I was much more satisfied and, I imagine, much more pleasant to deal with. After explaining the situation to him, he walked me through the same diagnostic procedures the previous person had. He paused for a few moments and said, "Mr. Belding, I have good news and bad news. The good news is that it can be fixed. The bad news is that I can't think of any way for us to repair your computer in time for your meeting tomorrow. If I was in your shoes, however, here's what I would try to recover your file . . ."

Unlike my conversation with the first representative, I found myself thanking this person for his efforts. And even though none of his suggestions worked, I felt as though he understood my challenge and was making an effort to solve the right problem.

If your callers are to be influenced, they must be confident that you understand them and their needs. If you can't convey that, then like the parent whose teenager has just shrieked "You just don't understand!" you have very little chance of exerting any influence on your callers.

Compassion

In the example above, the second TSR not only demonstrated to me that he comprehended my situation but also, through his tone of voice, effectively conveyed that he empathized with my situation. He demonstrated a sense of compassion. The ability to express compassion over the telephone is an absolutely invaluable skill when it comes to dealing with difficult callers.

If there is a common denominator with every difficult caller we get — that every irate, nasty, misbehaving caller has in common — it's that he or she believes we don't care. That's one of the reasons why callers are behaving so oddly and becoming so frustrated. Think about the first TSR in the experience I just described to you. My frustration was only in part a sense of "You just don't get it"; the other aspect was a clear feeling of "You just don't care."

When you recall the last poor service experience you had, whether it was on the phone or in person, what were the most notable parts of it? Chances are it was the person, not the issue, that made it an unpleasant experience. As we discussed earlier, it's typically a service-person's reaction to a situation, not the situation itself, that creates the most grief. And a big part of what makes us upset is when the serviceperson's reaction includes a perceived lack of caring. That old saying "No one cares how much you know, until they know how much you care," couldn't be more true.

Competence

Compassion and comprehension on their own, however, usually aren't enough to positively influence most callers. Understanding and sympathizing with the situation are very important, but the one question that will still be burning on your customer's mind is "Can you do anything about it?" Can you fix it? Can you diagnose it? Can you make your caller happy?

Competence is a critical component in creating influence. For your caller to begin feeling comfortable with you, he must believe that you have the capability to deal with his issue. If you can't send that message, you're almost guaranteed to get those dreaded words "May I speak to your supervisor please?"

We'll spend quite a bit of time in this book talking about how to convey competence to your caller. Most people go about it the wrong way and send completely wrong messages. Some launch into techno-babble, which makes people feel insecure. Others take a decidedly cool, snooty air, which alienates callers. The secret to coming across as being competent, as we will discover, is not to try to sound smarter but to learn how to ask the right questions at the right moments for the right reasons. People who try too hard just come across as . . . well . . . people who are trying too hard.

Confidence

The fourth C of influence is confidence. Projecting an air of confidence reassures your customer and makes her more confident in you and the company. People place great value on confidence — at least as much as they do on competence. Most people, in fact, equate the two, working on the assumption that, if someone appears confident, he or she must be competent. It's kind of like the relationship between product price and product quality. We generally tend to assume that, the more expensive something is, the better its quality.

Projecting an air of confidence can greatly influence your callers' trust in you and consequently their decisions. Not convinced? Imagine having the world's greatest heart surgeon preparing to do surgery on you, and the last words you hear before going under the anesthetic are "I hope I don't mess up." Now imagine the same scenario, this time with the world's fourth-best heart surgeon, who utters the words "This is going to go as smooth as silk." Which situation would make you the most comfortable? I think, if you're like most people, you'd pick fourth best any day.

Cheerfulness

To drive home the impact of these first four Cs of influence, think of this scenario. Imagine that your company has a new president. You discover that he has a tremendous amount of experience and knows the business inside out. He's done your job before, so he understands the unique challenges you face every day. He's very good at what he does and speaks in no uncertain terms about the direction in which he's taking the company. Is he a leader who might find himself with a lot of followers? Absolutely.

But there's one element — one C — left that will make the difference between someone who is an *effective* leader and someone who is a *charismatic* leader, the difference between someone you would trust, respect, and follow and someone who also *influences* you. That element is cheerfulness.

As I mentioned earlier, cheerfulness and being positive are closely related, and I'm introducing them twice because they are cornerstones to fundamental etiquette, as well as the keys to creating real influence with your caller. Cheerfulness is an integral component of charisma, and, the more charisma (or "Juice" as we call it in our seminars) that comes through on the telephone, the more influence you will have.

Cheerfulness, as it relates to charisma, does not necessarily mean that someone is always happy or jubilant. It means that her disposition is generally one of good cheer. A cheerful person enjoys life and people, is not afraid to laugh, and looks for the best in others. It is this disposition that makes the difference between people whom society perceives to be strong leaders and those whom we consider to be great or charismatic leaders. Churchill, Mandela, Gandhi, Reagan, Clinton, Trudeau, the Dalai Lama — love them or hate them, there has never been any question about their charisma and their influence on the people they led.

The Five Cs of Influence have a tremendous impact on your caller. If your caller perceives you as a competent, confident, compassionate, and cheerful person who comprehends the situation, he will feel as though he is in good hands. If he was planning on being a Customer from Hell, he's not likely to hit that heightened emotional state that comes with confrontation. If he was a potential customer, he will feel more comfortable doing business with you.

The next question, though, is how do you project these qualities over the telephone? Most people find themselves struggling to convey these five qualities live and in person, much less trying to project them in a one-dimensional, audio-only environment. The answer, of course, is tone of voice — that elusive sound quality that everyone is aware of but few truly master. We all talk about tone of voice ("Don't take that tone with me, young man!" "Tone it down a little!" "I don't like your tone!"), but what exactly is it? We all know what sarcasm sounds like — or panic, or happiness, or sullenness — but what are the actual changes in our voices that create these vivid messages? The better we can understand this, the far better communicators we all become. There is a great deal of research to suggest that tone of voice is equal to, and sometimes greater than, the actual words we choose to influence other people.

Speaking with SPLIT

So let's talk about tone of voice. When we think about good tone, we tend to think of those rich, basso profundo voices like those of James Earl Jones and Barry White. Their voices are distinctive primarily because they speak at a very low pitch. But if lower-pitched voices are truly more soothing and enjoyable, then why do people typically raise the pitch of their voices when talking to infants? Or why do men and women use higher tones when greeting each other and in courtship? The answer is that, while pitch is very important in creating good tone, it is only one of five controllable elements of tone. Five things that you can manipulate to change the meaning of your words. When we're teaching voice tone, we use the acronym SPLIT, which stands for speed, pitch, loudness, inflection, and timbre. These five things, when controlled properly, can very effectively replace the missing element of body language in your efforts to influence and persuade your callers. The following is an overview of each element and how you can develop it for greater results.

Speed

We've all seen the extremes — people who seem to speak a mile a minute and people who are so ponderously slow you just want to reach in and somehow wind them up. It's generally accepted that the average rate of speaking in the English language is between 125 and 150 words per minute. In 1969, researchers W. Foulke and T.G. Sticht determined that our ability to comprehend speech is actually almost double that rate. The theory as to why our conversational speed isn't faster is that this "extra" capacity allows our brains to comprehend what others are saying and simultaneously carry on an internal conversation — such as composing a response or evaluating information.

Want to test your rate of speaking? Read the following passage aloud, as though you were reading someone a story. (Don't read it silently — studies show that we read more than twice as fast as we speak.) Use the same kinds of inflections and pauses you would normally use. Use a watch or clock with a second hand and time yourself.

The young man walked down to the river's edge and watched the brilliant red sunset portend of good days to come. How long it would be before he too would have to leave, he couldn't guess. He only wished that when the day came, he would not be alone. What life would be like without Maria, he could not – no, would not – imagine.

But would she come with him? Would her mother and father allow it? His head filled with too many questions, and too few answers, so he slowly turned and began the long journey back to the village.

If you completed this 100-word passage in 40–50 seconds, then you're speaking at about the average rate of 125–50 words per minute. Anything below 35 seconds would be considered above average, and anything above 55 seconds would be considered below average.

Now, does this mean that if you speak at above-average speed you should slow down? Or that if you speak at below-average speed you should speed up? Does it mean that if you fall in the average range you shouldn't make any adjustments to your speech rate? Not exactly. This is just a guideline as to the optimal rate of speed as it relates to the comprehension of the words you are using. When it comes to using speed to influence or persuade, however, it's a very different story.

I've never actually measured it, but Michelle Quattrociocchi, Human Resources Manager for Tiens North America, has a natural speech rate that I'm sure is many times greater than average. Not all the time, of course, but when she begins to talk on a subject about which she is passionate I'm certain that she can go without breathing for several minutes. Having said this, however, I am absolutely confident that no one would ever contest her ability to make herself understood. I am equally confident that no one would ever doubt her passion or enthusiasm for what she does. And that's the key.

The relationship between her rate of speech and the way people perceive her — motivated, enthusiastic, and positive — is not an accident. Sure, if Michelle used that rate of speech while giving you a weather report, briefing you on a financial statement, or providing something else that required information only, your comprehension might be in jeopardy. But in those instances, I suspect, she would instinctively slow down and become more deliberate.

I don't know how much of her speaking skill is natural and how much is learned, but I do know that Michelle is a great communicator. And she knows, as all great communicators do, that speed is not a constant. It should be manipulated depending on the situation, what you are trying to project, and your audience. If you're trying to project enthusiasm and positive energy, a faster pace is the way to do it. And those are precisely the elements she injects into the workplace.

Rate of speech fluctuates as we speak. Some sentences move faster, and some are spoken more slowly. This is referred to as tempo, which is the rhythm of our speech. It is the difference between the teacher whose monotone droning put you to sleep and the one who kept you on the edge of your seat. It's the difference between the constantly shrill, over-hyping infomercial hawkers and powerful motivational speakers.

In addition to the fluctuations of speech rate, tempo is the combination of words and pauses that creates emphasis on specific ideas. It's the difference between "A woman without her man is nothing" and "A woman — without her, man is nothing," where the pauses created actually change the meaning of the sentence. Another example is "I've been meaning to tell you I love you" and "I've been meaning to tell you — I love you," where the pause changes the meaning from a perfunctory "Oh, by the way," to a heartfelt message.

Tempo is created through the variation of your rate of speech and the use of vocalized and nonvocalized pauses. Vocalized pauses are meaningless sounds that we use to fill in real pauses. Sounds such as "um," "er," "uh," "well," "like," and "you know" are common vocalized pauses. Although vocalized pauses are almost never recommended when speaking with someone, they do have a similar effect to silent pauses in changing the tempo of speech.

Learning how to vary your speech rate to create the right kind of tempo for the right kind of effect requires a lot of listening and a lot of practice. There are a number of other considerations to take into account when assessing what is an appropriate speech rate. Here are a few.

1. Age

Several studies have demonstrated that our ability to process auditory information slows as we age. A slower speaking speed — between 90 and 100 words per minute — is more appropriate for callers who are obviously seniors. Children, on the other hand, absorb auditory information faster and have shorter attention spans. This suggests a slightly faster speech rate.

2. Knowledge Level

If you're speaking with someone who is already knowledgeable about the subject, you can speak faster than you can with someone who is in the early learning stages. A technical support representative for a computer company has to dramatically slow his speech to work with someone who is new to computers. He can increase his speech rate, however, when dealing with someone who has a great deal of computer knowledge.

3. Message

The speed with which you speak should be appropriate to the complexity of the message you are delivering. If you have to give someone a lot of detailed information, speak more slowly (though not so slowly as to put them to sleep!). Similarly, if you are walking someone through a set of complex instructions, slow down. When the message is fairly straightforward, though, or you will be repeating it several times, your normal rate of speech is appropriate.

4. Language

I'll never forget conducting a customer service course many years ago in a small town in northern New Brunswick, Canada. Our client had sent us there, not realizing that close to 50% of the audience spoke only French and that English, for most of the others, was a second language. My training partner spoke no French at all, and mine was limited to inquiring as to where the washroom was. Unfortunately, we hadn't made this discovery until the participants were entering the room — so it was too late to postpone the session until we could bring in an appropriate bilingual trainer. After a quick strategy huddle, we decided to make a game of it. We recruited all of the bilingual people in the audience to be our translators, we cut out half the material, and we conducted the seminar at half speed. We had an absolute ball, and so did the participants. Everyone there learned something that day. Our participants learned a little more about customer service, and we learned how much people can comprehend in a second language when the speaker is patient and speaks at a rate they can process.

When you have callers for whom the language you are communicating in is a second language, slow down! They will appreciate it, and you will prevent a lot of miscommunication. We'll talk more about how to deal with language barriers in chapter thirteen.

In addition to tailoring your speaking rate to the nature of the message and your audience, keep in mind what you are trying to accomplish. Michelle, for example, is typically in a role in which she needs to portray herself and her company in a positive, proactive light — hence the appropriateness of her speech rate. Attempting to calm callers who are hysterical, however, requires speaking much more slowly and deliberately. The following is a simple chart identifying the correlation between speech rate and perception. Notice the correlation between voice speed and the Five Cs of Influence.

Perception	Speed
Angry	Slow or fast
Bored	Slow
Cheerful	Moderately fast
Compassionate	Average
Competent	Average to moderately fast
Confident	Average
Controlled, calm	Average
Enthusiastic	Fast
Friendly	Average
Happy	Average to moderately fast
Nervous	Fast
Sad	Slow
Sympathetic	Moderately slow
Thinking	Slow
Unsure	Slow

As you can see from the chart, your speech rate plays a significant role in your tone of voice and how you are perceived by your callers. You can also see that changing your rate of speech alone is not enough to clearly communicate an emotion. Speaking slowly can communicate boredom, sadness, being unsure, or thinking. Speaking quickly can communicate enthusiasm or nervousness. It's not until you begin to add in the other four elements of SPLIT that a voice tone becomes clearly defined.

Pitch

Voice pitch, or the frequency at which our voices resonate, plays a significant role in a caller's perception of us. At one level, research confirms that people who speak at lower pitches are ascribed generally more positive characteristics than those who speak at higher pitches. Lower-pitched voices are linked to confidence, truthfulness, and competence, while higher-pitched voices are linked to stress and nervousness. Research on advertising seems to support these findings, showing that low pitch, combined with a high speech rate, produces more favorable ad attitudes as well as more favorable brand attitudes.

Having said this, people who speak in higher-pitched voices are more likely to be perceived as enthusiastic, fun, eager, or creative, while people with lower-pitched voices can be perceived as serious, somber, and boring. Listen to people talking to infants and pets, for example, and you will notice a distinct rise in their pitch. This is because higher pitches are also perceived as more friendly and less threatening. By controlling your pitch, therefore, you can subtly influence how you are perceived. Let's take another look at the 15 perceived attributes we examined for voice speed as they relate to voice pitch.

Perception	Pitch
Angry	High
Bored	Low
Cheerful	High
Compassionate	Low
Competent	Average to low
Confident	Average to low
Controlled, calm	Average
Enthusiastic	High
Friendly	Average to high
Happy	Average to high
Nervous	High
Sad	Low
Sympathetic	Low
Thinking	Average to low
Unsure	Average

Again you can see how altering your pitch on its own can't send clear messages to your caller. A higher-pitched voice can imply that you are angry, nervous, enthusiastic, or cheerful. A lower-pitched voice can mean that you are bored, sad, sympathetic, or compassionate. As we start to put them together, however, we can see how the elements of speed and pitch begin sending messages to the person we are talking to.

Perception	Speed	Pitch
Angry	Slow or fast	High
Bored	Slow	Low
Cheerful	Moderately fast	High
Compassionate	Average	Low
Competent	Average to moderately fast	Average to low
Confident	Average	Average to low
Controlled, calm	Average	Average
Enthusiastic	Fast	High
Friendly	Average	Average to high
Happy	Average to moderately fast	Average to high
Nervous	Fast	High
Sad	Slow	Low
Sympathetic	Moderately slow	Low
Thinking	Slow	Average to low
Unsure	Slow	Average

In this chart, you can see how, by simply controlling two of the five elements, you can begin to better control the way in which your caller will perceive you.

There's more to controlling voice pitch than trying to keep your average pitch higher or lower, though. Controlling the fluctuations in your voice pitch throughout a sentence, or *intonation*, can also create impact. Consider the simple sentence "Good morning, sir," which contains three words and four syllables. Think of the different messages you can send simply by changing your intonation by syllable. In the following chart, each syllable is broken down into high-pitch, mid-pitch, and low-pitch to demonstrate the impacts that sound fluctuations have.

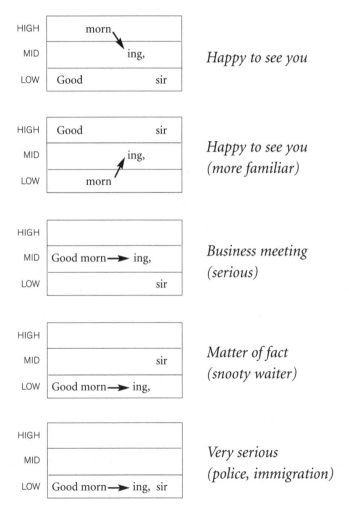

Happy to see you

*Happy to see you
(more familiar)*

*Business meeting
(serious)*

*Matter of fact
(snooty waiter)*

*Very serious
(police, immigration)*

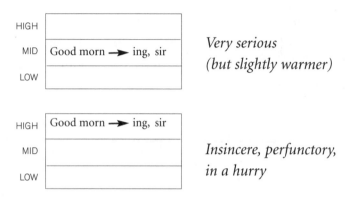

As we'll see in chapter thirteen, "Accents and Language Barriers," intonation is one of the most significant characteristics when dealing with accents. Improper intonation, or misreading the intonation of others, often causes unfortunate misunderstandings. Different languages have dramatically different intonations, and such variance easily leads to people saying the right things in the wrong ways. Intonation is also a common differentiation even between regional dialects, so misinterpretation can happen even between people speaking the same language.

Loudness

The loudness with which we speak, the sound volume, can be a strong signal of our emotional states. As a general rule, the more emotionally expressive we become (with either positive or negative emotions), the louder we get. Think of two people in an argument and how the sound volume gradually increases until both are shouting. The same two people winning the lottery would likely achieve a similar decibel level. It's also very common for people to be unaware of how loud they are. I think we have all, at some point, heard someone shout "I'm not shouting!"

If you're paying attention, a caller's speaking volume can be a good indicator of his emotional state, and you can track how well you're doing in dealing with a situation by tracking whether the caller becomes louder or quieter over time. It's also an attribute that you must become acutely aware of in your own voice because, consciously or unconsciously, your caller will also be monitoring your volume level. And if he detects an increase in how loudly you speak, he can perceive you as becoming agitated or less flexible.

To understand the impact of loudness, it might help to think of the body language analogy of how close you stand to someone in a conversation. Speaking loudly is analogous to standing nose to nose with someone, while speaking quietly is comparable to standing some distance away. On the one hand, people who close in on our "personal space" may be perceived as being stronger and more confident; on the other hand, they may be perceived as being insensitive bullies. Similarly, people who create too great a distance can be perceived as less threatening and more agreeable or, conversely, as aloof and uncaring.

Let's take another look at our chart, this time adding in the loudness factor.

Perception	Speed	Pitch	Loudness
Angry	Slow or fast	High	Loud
Bored	Slow	Low	Quiet
Cheerful	Moderately fast	High	Moderately loud
Compassionate	Average	Low	Average to quiet
Competent	Average to moderately fast	Average to low	Average
Confident	Average	Average to low	Average to moderately loud
Controlled, calm	Average	Average	Moderately quiet to quiet
Enthusiastic	Fast	High	Loud
Friendly	Average	Average to high	Average
Happy	Average to moderately fast	Average to high	Average to moderately loud
Nervous	Fast	High	Loud or quiet
Sad	Slow	Low	Quiet
Sympathetic	Moderately slow	Low	Quiet
Thinking	Slow	Average to low	Quiet
Unsure	Slow	Average	Moderately quiet

Now we are starting to get a picture of how the elements of voice tone work together to send messages about who we are. The loudness with which you speak can signal different things to your caller depending on the topic. For instance, loudly saying "Sir, you will not be getting a refund," will come across as confrontational and negative. However, loudly saying "Sir, I think you deserve a refund," can come across as though you are championing the caller's cause. Another example might be if you were to quietly say "I'm not sure if I can do that for you," which could come across as indecisive and not confident. Quietly saying "I am truly sorry this happened to you," however, will come across as sincere and compassionate.

Learning to control how loudly you speak is difficult because of the difficulty in hearing yourself with any degree of objectivity. In our voice control workshops, we bring in a sound meter so that people can discover exactly what their decibel ranges are. In every group, there is usually one person who speaks a little louder and one who speaks a little softer. Each is typically surprised at how dramatic the differences really are. To give an idea as to what average speaking volumes are, and how they compare to other sounds, we use this decibel intensity chart from *Encarta 2005*:

0 – threshold of hearing

10 – rustle of leaves, a quiet whisper

20 – average whisper

20–50 – quiet conversation

40–45 – hotel, theater between performances

50–65 – loud conversation

65–70 – traffic on a busy street

65–90 – train

75–80 – factory noise (light/medium work)

90 – heavy traffic

90–100 – thunder

110–40 – jet aircraft at takeoff

130 – threshold of pain

140–90 – space rocket on takeoff

Inflection

Perhaps the single most powerful tool we have to send messages with our voices is inflection — the emphasis we put on different words in a sentence. With subtle changes in inflection, the three simple words "Nice job, Alicia," could be high praise or dark sarcasm. Or think, for example, of the statement "I didn't say he could do that" and the changes in meaning you can create simply by changing which word you put the emphasis on.

- *I* didn't say he could do that. (Someone else did.)
- I *didn't* say he could do that. (I deny saying that.)

- I didn't *say* he could do that. (I implied it.)
- I didn't say *he* could do that. (I said someone else could do it.)
- I didn't say he *could* do that. (I said he should do it.)
- I didn't say he could *do* that. (I said he could tell people about it.)
- I didn't say he could do *that*. (I said he could do something else.)

Inflection, although I have identified it here separately, is really the use of pitch (intonation), volume, and tempo on specific words within a sentence. Saying "I didn't say he could do that," for example, with the word *didn't* spoken more loudly, with a higher pitch, and with a slight pause afterward creates a distinctive "defensive denial" message. Inflection, as with intonation, plays a significant role in accents. For people who teach second languages, this is often the most difficult aspect to teach, because it is learned more through experience than through specific rules. As a general guideline, however, the emphasis should always be put on the most important word in the sentence — the word to which you want to direct the most attention.

In many instances, when dealing with the Caller from Hell, we need to adopt what is referred to as a "neutral tone." A neutral tone means that you speak without any inflection at all, and it is more difficult than it may seem. The intention is to create a tone of voice that minimizes the danger of misinterpretation or of people "reading between the lines."

Timbre

When we try to define the timbre, the "color" or "quality" of someone's voice, we typically resort to analogies and descriptive words. Warm, clear, bright, mellow, soothing, whiny, dark, thin, strident, full are just some of the words we use. Unfortunately, these words don't give us much of a clue about how these sounds are created or how we can manipulate vocal timbre to achieve different effects.

To understand timbre, and how to manipulate it, it helps to have an understanding of how the vocal system works. There are three basic components to your voice: the source of airflow, the source of sound, and the source of sound modification. In physiological terms, it's your lungs, your larynx, and your vocal tract. Your lungs create the power by pushing air up into your larynx. The muscles in your larynx change the length and thickness of your vocal cords, which create sound. Your vocal tract — your oral and nasal cavities — is where the sound is manipulated into words and sound quality.

There are five basic categories of voice sounds: breathy, nasal, forward, throaty, and resonant. Breathy, when quiet, is referred to as a "whisper" and when louder may be referred to as "sexy." Nasal is when the air is pushed more through the nose, creating a "thinner" sound. The voices of actor Fran Drescher and *Sesame*

Street's Snuffleupagus are examples of higher- and lower-pitched nasal vocalizations. Forward is when the sound is produced primarily in the mouth, such as when adults engage in "baby talk." Throaty is when the sound is colored deeper in the throat, much like Disney's Goofy character. Resonant is the clear, powerful sound when the airflow is generated by the diaphragm and is balanced between the nasal and oral cavities. Professional news announcers, singers, and speakers have resonant voices.

Does the timbre of your voice impact how you're perceived or your ability to influence callers? Absolutely. Let's revisit our chart and see how timbre fits in.

Perception	Speed	Pitch	Loudness	Timbre
Angry	Slow or fast	High	Loud	Forward
Bored	Slow	Low	Quiet	Nasal
Cheerful	Moderately fast	High	Moderately loud	Resonant
Compassionate	Average	Low	Average to quiet	Resonant
Competent	Average to moderately fast	Average to low	Average	Resonant
Confident	Average	Average to low	Average to moderately loud	Resonant
Controlled, calm	Average	Average	Moderately quiet to quiet	Resonant
Enthusiastic	Fast	High	Loud	Resonant, forward
Friendly	Average	Average to high	Average	Resonant

Perception	Speed	Pitch	Loudness	Timbre
Happy	Average to moderately fast	Average to high	Average to moderately loud	Resonant
Nervous	Fast	High	Loud or quiet	Forward, breathy
Sad	Slow	Low	Quiet	Throaty
Sympathetic	Moderately slow	Low	Quiet	Resonant
Thinking	Slow	Average to low	Quiet	Throaty
Unsure	Slow	Average	Moderately quiet	Nasal, forward

Generally speaking, there's a lot of benefit in trying to develop a resonant vocal timbre. It gives you a great deal more control and allows you to more effectively project a wider range of emotions. You can see by the chart that most positive outcomes require a resonant timbre.

Our voices are amazing instruments, with a range and a flexibility unlike anything else. We can control our speed, pitch, loudness, inflection, and timbre to achieve quite astonishing results. Like any other skill, though, voice control requires diligent practice. People who take our speaking and listening workshops are always surprised at how much of a difference vocal changes make in an interaction.

As with any other valuable instrument, our voices also require care and attention. Smoking, alcohol, caffeine, yelling — all can damage your vocal cords. If you are on the telephone all day, drink plenty of water. A little lemon in the water can be good. Avoid coffee and tea (with the exception of decaffeinated or herbal teas). Don't smoke, and try to keep your work area well humidified (but not damp). In the mornings, before you go to work, try some vocalization exercises to warm your voice up. Go through the scales (do, re, mi, fa, so, la, ti, do). Press your hand to your stomach and say "Ha! Ha! Ha!" Your stomach should push against your hand to confirm that you are using your diaphragm. If you are really serious about mastering your voice, take a course such as our Speaking & Listening workshop. Join a choral organization, such as your church choir, a barbershop chorus, Sweet Adelines, or Harmony Incorporated. They are great ways to learn how to use and develop your voice.

Whatever you do, don't ignore it. And remember — if you find yourself with customers responding negatively to the things you say, it's possible that it isn't what you are saying at all but the way in which you are saying it.

Here, again, are the Five Cs of Influence and SPLIT, the five elements of voice tone that you can control.

The Five Cs of Influence

Comprehension

Compassion

Competence

Confidence

Cheerfulness

Controlling Voice Tone with SPLIT

Speed

Pitch

Loudness

Inflection

Timbre

CHAPTER FOUR

ACTUALLY, IT IS WHAT YOU SAY . . .

The language of diplomacy is critical when
doing business over the telephone,
and bluntness rarely achieves a positive effect.

I was listening to calls in a cellular telephone company's call center, trying to determine why certain people seemed to have more than their share of difficult callers and why some seemed to have less. Were some people just unfortunate to be receiving a disproportionate number of Callers from Hell, or was it something else? As you might expect, tone of voice played a significant role in how customers reacted to the CSRs. The most significant distinction between the CSRs with a lot of Callers from Hell and those with few Callers from Hell, however, was in their actual choice of words.

One of the common "difficult caller" issues that CSRs were dealing with in this call center was people calling in to order a free phone. It was available to anyone who'd been with the company for more than two years and who was willing to commit to a two-year contract. There were a number of restrictions in the small print, one of which was that clients had to be current in their payments. This wouldn't have been much of a challenge for most people except that the company was notorious for getting bills out late, thereby making it difficult for people to stay current.

Following are some of the things I heard from the CSRS. See if you can guess which ones were well received by customers and which ones weren't.

A. You're going to have to get your payments up to date before we can send you a phone.

B. I'm sorry, but you can't have the phone until you've paid your bill.

C. It looks like your account might be slightly behind. We can send you the phone just as soon as all the payments are caught up.

D. Absolutely I can get you your free phone. We'll need you to get a payment in for your September bill, but as soon as it's in the phone will be shipped to you right away.

E. Sir, it looks like you have an overdue payment. There's no point in ordering your phone now. You should make the payment and then call us back.

F. Ms. Johnson, I've just noticed that your account isn't quite up to date. Just so you're aware, there may be a delay in receiving your phone, until everything is back to normal.

We found that CSRS who used statements similar to A, B, and E more often triggered negative responses than CSRS who used statements similar to C, D, and F. But what is the difference? And how is it that such subtle language changes can trigger such dramatically different responses in our callers?

The fact is that our choices of words and phrases play a huge role in both averting and resolving conflict. The language of diplomacy is critical when doing business over the telephone, and bluntness rarely achieves a positive effect. The secret is to speak in such a manner as to minimize the number of negative hot buttons you push in people and to increase the number of positive hot buttons. As the late crooner Bing Crosby used to sing, "You've got to accentuate the positive / Eliminate the negative / . . . Don't mess with Mister In-Between."

Hot Buttons

Like it or not, we all have hot buttons that can repeatedly trigger specific emotions when pushed — emotions that can range from positive and happy to negative and angry. They are different for all of us, and one of the greatest mistakes you can make is to assume that everyone is motivated by the same stimuli you are. There seem to be as many hot buttons as there are people, and, try as I might, I have yet to be able to predict what someone's hot buttons will be before I talk with that person. Here are some hot buttons I've seen over the years.

Statement/question:	How much did you want to spend?
Hot button:	He thinks I'm poor.
Statement/question:	Can I see another piece of ID?
Hot button:	He thinks I'm trying to cheat him.
Statement/question:	It's pretty expensive – about $100.
Hot button:	He thinks I'm cheap.
Statement/question:	You'll have to wait.
Hot button:	He thinks I'm not very important.
Statement/question:	This is very popular with women.
Hot button:	He thinks I'm gullible because I'm a woman.
Statement/question:	It was an African American man wearing a blue shirt.
Hot button:	He's using racial profiling.
Statement/question:	I own a pit bull.
Hot button:	He's irresponsible.

Hot buttons aren't necessarily right or wrong. Nor are they always based on rational thought. They are simply triggers that create an emotional response in us. Some words, just on their own, can trigger emotional responses. Research shows that, even with no context, simple words such as *feminist, freedom, political, racial,* and *radical* can spawn strong positive or negative emotions within people. Another recent study showed how differently people are affected by the word *crash* as opposed to words such as *accident, collision,* or *incident.*

The media are famous for using hot-button words to

evoke responses from us. Use of the word *crash*, as I mentioned above, is just one of the words they can pull out of their bag of hot-button tricks. Another example is use of the word *secret*. If a city council, for instance, has an in-camera, or private, meeting to discuss a sensitive issue, the headlines in the papers will inevitably refer to a "secret" meeting. We don't even have to read the article to begin forming the opinion that city council has done something wrong.

In chapter six, we'll discuss in more detail how to prevent callers from pushing your hot buttons, but let's take a look at how you can reduce the odds of tramping on the minefield of random hot buttons your callers have hidden away in their brains. To accomplish this, you need a basic understanding of positive and "gentle" language as well as sensitivity to and empathy with your caller. The first comes with practice, the second two with listening.

Positive Language

Positive language, as the name suggests, is using language focused on positive things instead of negative things. It's language that is less likely to elicit a negative response. Gentle language is words and phrases that are less blunt and more diplomatic. Learning to use positive and gentle language begins with trying to avoid negative words and phrases. Following are a few negative words and phrases that often have the effect of pushing people's hot buttons. You'll find that it really pays off to avoid them.

Yergunnahafta

"Yergunnahafta talk to my supervisor." "Yergunnahafta wait." "Yergunnahafta call someone else." "Yergunnahafta send your computer in." "Yergunnahafta speak louder." Yergunnahafta may be the most annoying "word" in the English language. Remember this always — your callers don't "gunnahafta" do anything.

Problem

If there is a word that has no place in our language, it's *problem*. Most of us have heard the saying "There's no such thing as problems — just opportunities and challenges." But few of us actually embrace the concept. The fact is, if you can get in the habit of using the words *challenge* and *opportunity* instead of *problem*, you'll discover that problem becomes an absolutely unnecessary word.

Don't think it makes a difference? Imagine for a moment three people running a cross-country race. They find themselves neck and neck running through a trail in the woods. As they run out of the woods, there in front of them is a huge mountain, with the trail going straight up to the peak. They all stop and look at it. The first runner smiles and says, "Now *there's* a challenge!" The second runner says, "I've never climbed a mountain before — what an opportunity!" The third sighs and says, "Now *there's* a problem!" Who will win the race? I don't know for sure, but I have a pretty good idea who's going to lose it. Drop the word *problem* from your vocabulary. You won't miss it.

No Problem

The phrase *no problem* has become a common part of our vernacular. Unfortunately, it's replaced the perfectly good words *yes, absolutely, thank you,* and *you're welcome.* For some reason, we seem to be intent on replacing positive words with a negative phrase. If your caller wasn't expecting a problem, why would you want to tell her she's not going to have one?

Yabut

"Yabut, that's not the way we do things." "Yabut, yergunnahafta do this first." "Yabut, I wouldn't recommend it." Yabut, yabut, yabut. Anyone who has kids knows the word *yabut,* and it's no less annoying when we adults say it. Yabut ("Yes, but") — in fact, any phrase with the word *but* in it — should be avoided at all costs. For all intents and purposes, *but* means "ignore everything I just said, because now I'm going to tell you what I'm really thinking."

You Don't Understand

Saying "You don't understand" to most people is like waving a red flag to a bull. The underlying message that can come across is "You're stupid" — not something anyone likes to hear. The phrase also places the burden of miscommunication directly on the caller, suggesting that it is somehow all her fault that there is a lack of understanding. A better way of expressing this is to say something like "I think I'm not communicating this well." This phrasing still indicates that there is a misunderstanding but is less likely to push a caller's button because you have put the responsibility for the failed communication on yourself.

You're Wrong

Telling someone that she is wrong, or even telling her that you think she is wrong, is an almost guaranteed button-pusher. Try these sentences instead: "That's not my understanding," "There may be some aspects of this that you're not aware of," or "I'm not convinced that's entirely the case." Each of these alternative statements has removed the personification of "you're." In using this approach, you remove much of the need for your caller to become defensive.

Using positive and gentle language means thinking before you speak. Is there a better way to say this? What do I want the outcome to be? Could this upset someone? This is a particularly important skill to have when you're in a situation where you have to present something negative. Let's take a look at how different statements can be reworded more gently and positively.

Negative: Yergunnahafta get this fixed before you can use it again.

Positive: You'll be able to use it again just as soon as you fix this one thing.

Negative: This is totally unacceptable. It's nowhere near being up to standard.

Positive: Here are the things we have to do to get it up to standard.

Negative: You can't do it that way.

Positive: Here's the accepted way to do it.

Negative: I'm calling to see if there are any problems with your service.

Positive: I'm calling to make sure that you are completely satisfied with your service.

Negative: If you don't like the bill, yergunnahafta take it up with someone else.

Positive: Let me find the right person for you to speak with about this.

Negative: Yergunnahafta call customer service for that.

Positive: Customer service will be able to help you much faster. Let me connect you.

Negative: I can't do that.

Positive: Let me tell you what I can do.

Negative: There are some problems with your credit.

Positive: Your credit history indicates some challenges.

Negative: This is going to be a problem.

Positive: Let's see how we can make this work.

Every now and then I meet someone who likes to say "I'm a very honest person. I just tell it like it is." Inevitably, what the person really means is "I'm blunt, and I don't care if I hurt someone else's feelings." By convincing herself that she is "honest," she believes that she doesn't have to be sensitive. Unfortunately, the unwillingness to make the effort of using more positive and gentle language inevitably results in increased conflict later on. As we discussed at the beginning of the book, the majority of conflict is actually created by the serviceperson and not the caller. And failure to use positive and gentle language is one of the biggest culprits.

We talked about some of our caller's negative hot buttons to avoid, but what about their positive hot buttons? Are there any common messages we can use that will trigger positive responses? Absolutely. Here are a few positive hot buttons that can help you to increase your odds of having a positive experience with a caller.

You're Important

One thing we all have in common is that, at some level, we like to believe that we're important. That we are valued. Nobody enjoys the status of being "just another caller." No one wants to feel insignificant. Anything you can say or do that communicates to your caller that she is important will have a long-lasting positive effect. You don't even have to be subtle — just come right out and say it: "Your business is very important to us, Ms. Kellerman," or "You are a very important customer, Ms. Marsden."

I Care

Empathy is one of the fastest ways to build a connection with a caller — particularly when the caller is facing a challenge. So in addition to saying "Your business is very important to us, Ms. Kellerman," don't hesitate to add

"It's important to me that you're satisfied." There are many different ways to exhibit empathy, but when we are on the telephone the absence of body language restricts us somewhat. To compensate, use verbal prompts such as "Oh, no!" or "Oh, dear!" or "How terrible!"

I'm Interested
The best way to communicate to your caller that you are genuinely interested in who he is and why he's called is to pay attention to him. To listen. We'll talk more about this in chapter eight. It's also important your caller get the message that you're willing to help (even if sometimes you're unable to). A sincere "Mr. Neilson, what can I do to help?" will send the message, loudly and clearly, that you are interested in resolving the situation.

I'm Not Judging You
One of the greatest sources of discomfort with callers who have to speak with you about sensitive issues — financial, health, occupational, or family issues — is the fear of being judged. And a lot of times the odd behavior that you encounter with callers is simply a related defensive mechanism. You need to communicate early on that, regardless of what the call is about, you aren't passing judgment on your callers.

This is best accomplished by maintaining the warmest possible tone of voice under the circumstances.

Try not to be abrupt or to come across as cool. Keep the yergunnahaftas to a minimum, and use gentle language. When someone offers an excuse or explanation, don't ignore it or discount it. Give the caller feedback with words and phrases that convey empathy, such as "Oh, no!" or "Really?" or "How horrible!"

If you can master voice control and the use of specific words and phrases to better control which of a caller's hot buttons you're pushing, you'll go a long way in reducing a lot of conflict. Combine those skills with a consistent use of the fundamental practices of etiquette outlined in chapter two and you can almost be assured that any conflict you face isn't one of your own making. The secret, now, is to learn how to effectively control a call to ensure that it doesn't go off track.

Here, again, are five negative words and phrases you should avoid and four positive sentiments you should always try to communicate.

Avoid saying

1. Yergunnahafta. . . .
2. Problem. . . .
3. No problem. . . .
4. You don't understand. . . .
5. You're wrong. . . .

Communicate instead

1. You're important. . . .
2. I care. . . .
3. I'm interested. . . .
4. I'm not judging you. . . .

THE MOST IMPORTANT COMMUNICATION SKILL YOU WILL EVER LEARN

When we simply answer a caller's questions, with no follow-up, we become no more than directory information or an on-line brochure.

I was originally going to give this chapter the simple title of "Call Control," because that's what it's really all about. But the simple title just didn't do this skill justice. Call control — fundamental conversation control — is the most powerful yet least used communication skill there is. It's not terribly hard to understand, and most people can master it with a little time and practice. It's unfortunate that so few people make the effort to become good at it.

What is call control? It's the process of being able to direct the flow, focus, and tone of a conversation. It's the ability to ensure that the conversation remains on track and that you are able to deal with issues efficiently and effectively. Just as doctors have control when conducting examinations, lawyers have control when deposing witnesses on the stand, and talk-show hosts have control in their interviews, CSRs need to be able to take control when a customer calls them.

Why is it important that we control a call? Why not just let the caller take control? Well, the truth is you can. And that is precisely what most people do. Most of us are content to answer our callers' questions and respond to their needs and moods. And as a result, we often find ourselves with that unsettling sense of calls "going sideways." The conversation gets off topic, callers ramble on, and we find ourselves solving the wrong problems. Imagine what could happen if doctors were to let us take control of our checkups.

Patient:	My side hurts.
Doctor:	Really?
Patient:	Do you think I have a broken rib?
Doctor:	No, I don't think so.
Patient:	Should we take an x-ray?
Doctor:	Probably not necessary.
Patient:	Could it be cancer?
Doctor:	I doubt it.
Patient:	Should I have an MRI?
Doctor:	No.
Patient:	Could it be my spleen?
Doctor:	Your spleen is on the other side. . . .

You can see how, with the patient in control, a checkup would take much longer than when the doctor is in control. Why should the doctor be in control? Because he's the expert.

You Are an Expert

In my customer service seminars, I often ask all the participants who believe themselves to be experts to raise their hands. Few, if any, ever do. "Why not?" I ask. The answer is always the same: there's a lot more they still have to learn, there are people out there who know more than they do, and so on. "Okay, so who are our experts?" I continue, and we spend three to four minutes making a list of people such as surgeons, accountants, professors, engineers, et cetera. "So," I continue, "are you telling me that your accountant knows everything there is to know about accounting? Or that a surgeon knows everything there is to know about surgery?" The answer, of course, is "No," to which I ask, "So what makes these individuals more of an expert than you?" The answer, inevitably, is silence.

"Expert," according to *Merriam Webster's Collegiate Dictionary*, is "having, involving, or displaying special skill or knowledge derived from training or experience." Chances are, unless you are just a few days on the job, *you are more of an expert than your customer*. You are your customers' expert. You know more about your products or services than your callers do. That's why they called you. And just as you would expect your doctor, surgeon, accountant, or lawyer to take control in matters pertaining to their expertise, you need to take control in the situations in which you are the expert.

So how do you take control of a conversation? Is the person in control the one who talks the most or the loudest? Absolutely not. Take a look at the doctor-patient example I used above, and you'll see that the person who was in control was the one asking the questions. And that is the rule for controlling any conversation, whether it is on the telephone or in person: *the person who asks the questions controls the conversation.*

The Power of Questions

Questions are wonderful things, and most people are largely unaware of the power questions possess. The person asking the questions decides which topic is being focused on, whether the focus is negative or positive, and which items are important or unimportant. The person who asks the questions inevitably becomes the center of focus as people are forced to respond to him. The person who asks the questions controls the outcome of a conversation.

I have a friend who is tremendously adept at asking

questions, and, when he's feeling a little mischievous, he uses this technique to torment salespeople. I remember standing with him in a large department store listening to a conversation between him and a salesperson desperately trying to sell him a vacuum cleaner. The salesperson had just completed his 10-minute pitch about why this one particular vacuum was better than the others. My friend picked up the vacuum cleaner in his hands, turned it around a few times, and said, "What is its energy efficiency like?" The salesperson floundered for a moment. It wasn't a question he knew the answer to. He tried to change the subject, but my friend persisted. When the salesperson attempted to duck the question a second time, my friend responded with "Why don't you want to answer my question about this vacuum cleaner's energy efficiency?" The salesperson twitched a little; then after a few moments' thought he suggested that he suspected it didn't likely consume more energy than any other vacuum. "How can that be?" my friend asked incredulously. "How can it be so much more powerful, as you claim, yet not use more power?" The salesperson was stumped and muttered something about a more efficient system. My friend jumped in again and said, "But you talked about how it has all those additional features. How can it have all those features and be more efficient?" The salesperson had reached full-fledged panic mode at this point as he saw the sale slipping away from him. "I . . . I really don't know," he finally mumbled. The aggressive sales pitch had totally disappeared as a result of a few well-placed questions.

Now, I'm not suggesting that you should, like my friend, use questions to torment innocent salespeople, but you can see the power they give you when you use them properly. My friend didn't really care about energy efficiency, but by asking questions about it he elevated its importance over the features the salesperson had been promoting. He effectively changed the direction of the conversation, and the hapless salesperson had no choice but to follow along.

When dealing with issues over the telephone, questions are an invaluable tool. By questioning your caller, you can create a funnel effect, moving from the general to the more specific, narrowing things down to identify and fine-tune issues and solutions. If you ever played the game 20 Questions as a child, you'll recognize the process.

For those of you who haven't played it, the rules are simple. Participants can ask 20 questions to identify what the one player is thinking of. The questions can only be in a "choice" format ("Is it a person, place, or thing?") or in a "closed-ended" format, in which the answer can only be either "Yes" or "No." The strategy for winning 20 Questions is to become adept at beginning with broad questions and gradually becoming more specific. Here's an example.

Question 1: Is it a person, place, or thing?

Answer: A thing.

Question 2: Is it bigger than a breadbox?

Answer: No.

Question 3: Do I have one?

Answer: Yes.

Question 4: Is it in my house?

Answer: Yes.

Question 5: Would it be in the basement?

Answer: No.

Question 6: Would it be on the main floor?

Answer: Yes.

Question 7: Would it be in the living room?

Answer: No.

Question 8: Would it be in the kitchen?

Answer: Yes.

Question 9: Can you eat it?

Answer: Yes.

Question 10: Would it be in the refrigerator?

Answer: Yes.

Question 11: Is it a liquid?

Answer: No.

Question 12: Is it a kind of meat?

Answer: No.

Question 13: Is it a vegetable?

Answer: Yes.

Question 14: Is it green?

Answer: Yes.

Question 15: Is it lettuce?

Answer: Yes.

In this example, the questioner progressed from the general "Is it a person, place, or thing?" to the specific "Is it lettuce?" in 15 questions. To illustrate the benefit of using this funnel approach, imagine how many questions she might have to ask if she doesn't use it.

Is it drywall?

No.

Is it an elephant?

No.

Is it ice cream?

No.

Is it Susan?

No. . . .

You can clearly see how, without using the funnel technique, the questions could go on indefinitely.

The game of 20 Questions illustrates another critical component of asking questions. While you control a conversation by asking questions, it's far more effective when you use *open-ended* questions. A question is open-ended when it requires an answer more complex than a simple "Yes" or "No." Open-ended questions always begin with one of six words, identified in the famous quotation by Rudyard Kipling:

> I keep six honest serving-men
> (They taught me all I knew);
> Their names are What and Why and When
> And How and Where and Who.

What, why, when, how, where, and who. Now imagine playing 20 Questions using open-ended questions. It would be the most boring game ever invented.

Question 1: What are you thinking of?
Answer: Lettuce.

It's a great illustration, though, of how one well-placed, open-ended question can replace 15 closed-ended questions.

Learning how to ask questions takes practice, and most people don't realize how limited their existing skills are until they start working at them. In our workshops, we often ask participants how many believe they ask a lot of questions of their callers. Virtually everyone raises his or her hand. We follow up with an exercise of having them write down as many open-ended questions as they can think of that they may need to deal with any situation with a caller. We're going to create a database of questions, we tell them, to use as a teaching tool for others. Predictably, the participants quickly begin to realize how few questions they can generate off the tops of their heads, and their combined lists rarely exceed 15 questions.

"Yabut this is different," the inevitable outcry ensues. "It's harder when we're just sitting here. When we have a caller on the line, it comes much more easily."

Nonsense.

The North American mystery shopping company, RetailTrack Mystery Shopping, reports that most customer service reps and salespeople ask fewer than three questions of their customers — and that number includes the ubiquitous and unproductive "Can I help you?" The fact is that most of us spend our time answering questions, not asking them.

The Opening Question Trap

In all fairness, one reason we end up with customers controlling conversations is that we fall into an insidious trap right from the beginning of a call. In the majority of cases, the first thing a caller does is ask a question. Here's a list of common customer opening lines in just a few different industries.

Calling a car rental agency

- Do you have any cars available?
- How much are your cars?
- What types of cars do you have available?
- What are your weekend rates?

Calling a cellular phone company

- I have a question regarding my bill. . . .
- How do I use the . . . feature?
- What kinds of plans do you have?

Calling an airline

- When is your next flight to. . . ?
- How much is a round-trip ticket to. . . ?
- When is the cheapest time to fly to. . . ?

Calling a pizza store

- Do you deliver?
- How much is a large supreme?
- How long would it take you to deliver a pizza?

Think about your own business. What are the questions that callers typically begin with?

When you think about what's happening from a control point of view, it's actually an interesting, albeit subconscious, phenomenon. Simply by asking the first question, you establish that you are in control by asking the first question, whether it's "Can I help you?" or just a simple "Yes?" Your caller, however, immediately wrestles control away from you by asking you a question: "How do I get my computer to work?" It's no wonder that so many calls go sideways with the nonexpert taking control so early on.

Now, I'm not suggesting that this is somehow wrong of our customers or that we should discourage them from asking questions — quite the opposite. Your customer's initial question is critical to the process. What I am suggesting, however, is that we are usually in a position right off the bat in which we need to reestablish control of the call.

Let's talk about the first question your caller asks. The purpose of her question is not some control-freak device for establishing dominance. It is, instead, simply the preferred method of introducing a topic. Think about what a caller is really trying to say when she asks a question. For example, when someone asks "How much are your cars?" what she is really communicating to you are *I need to rent a car* and *price is a consideration*. When a caller asks "Do you deliver?" he is also communicating two things to you: *I want a pizza* and *I need it delivered*.

It is important to understand what is really behind a caller's first question, because failure to do so can mean both missed opportunity and the potential for conflict. When we simply answer a caller's questions, with no follow-up, we become no more than directory information or an on-line brochure, which is not what the caller wanted. The caller is communicating her needs to you, and wants you, the expert, to take over from there.

Answer a Question, Ask a Question

The secret to maintaining control of a call is to learn the art of answering a question and then following up with a question of your own — just as the pizza person does in the following example.

Caller:	Do you deliver?
Pizza dude:	Absolutely! What can I get for you today?

Makes sense, doesn't it? So why wouldn't we do the same thing in other contexts?

Caller:	What types of cars do you have?
Car rental dude:	We have X,Y, and Z models. When do you need your car?
Caller:	When is your next flight to. . . ?
Airline dude:	Tomorrow at 8 a.m. How many people will be flying?
Caller:	What kinds of plans do you have?
Cell dude:	We have a number of plans. How often do you use your cell phone?

I'll never forget listening to a caller who called about her cellular telephone account. She began by asking the CSR what plan she was on. The CSR told her. She asked if the company had plans that offered free evenings and weekends. The CSR said yes and told her the rate. She asked if the company had plans where two people could share minutes. The CSR said yes, but they weren't available with free evenings and weekends. She asked if the company had any plans that offered free text messaging. The CSR said no, but the company had some plans where she could receive a certain number of messages for free. She asked if the company had a plan that offered long-distance rates. The CSR said yes but not in shared minute plans or free evening and weekend plans.

As I listened, I began to keep track of the number of questions the caller asked compared with the number the CSR asked. By the time the conversation wound down, and the thoroughly confused customer had said "Okay, well, I'll think about it and get back to you," the score was 16-1 for the caller. The one question the CSR had asked? "Hello, thank you for calling . . . , this is Amy speaking, how may I help you?"

For many people in sales, one of the biggest frustrations is what they refer to as "tire kickers": people who ask a lot of questions, take up a lot of valuable time, and then don't buy anything. I've spent over 15 years coaching and observing salespeople both over the telephone and in person. And I can state unequivocally that the vast majority of tire kickers could be converted to paying customers simply by having a "salesperson kicker" reminding the salesperson to take control and start asking the right questions.

Want to improve your question-asking skill and have a little fun in the process? Find a coworker and play the following game. Pick a topic that's relevant to your business. One of you be the caller and the other the CSR (whatever your occupation is). The caller begins by asking a question. The CSR has to answer it, then ask a relevant follow-up question. The caller then answers the CSR's question and asks another of his own. The first person to become stumped loses. After a few questions, it begins to get a little silly, but that's half the fun. Despite the silliness, however, it's a great way to practice an invaluable skill. Here's an example of how it might go.

Caller: Do you have a plan that offers free evenings and weekends?

CSR: Absolutely! Who is the plan for?

Caller: My wife and daughter and I. Can we share minutes?

CSR: Absolutely, although not with the free evening and weekend plan. Which would be more important to you?

Caller: They're both important. Can I get one of them with a long-distance plan?

> **CSR:** Sure, you can share minutes with a long-distance plan. How often do you make long-distance calls?
>
> **Caller:** All the time. How many calls can I make?
>
> **CSR:** It depends on the plan you choose. How much time do you suppose the three of you would need?

For two people who are good at this skill, the game can go on for quite some time. It's fun to listen to — kind of like a verbal table-tennis game with the control going back and forth. You will find, however, that people who are unpracticed will begin to struggle almost immediately.

Learning how to ask skillful, directed questions has far-reaching applications at work and at home. As you master this skill, you'll encounter fewer challenges with customers, coworkers, and bosses and find fewer situations you can't handle. It's worth a try — don't you think?

CHAPTER SIX

MANAGING YOUR EMOTIONAL STATES

While conflict is an inevitable component in dealing with large numbers of people, confrontation is not.

We've talked a little about Callers from Hell, what makes them tick, and basic etiquette and environment considerations for minimizing the number of times we shoot ourselves in the feet. We've talked about how to use our voices and language and questioning skills to maximize our opportunities for creating positive, proactive experiences. We've learned how to push the right hot buttons and avoid pushing the wrong hot buttons. The last skill in preparing to deal with Callers from Hell is to learn how to manage our emotional states.

It's pretty near impossible to hide our emotions. No matter how hard we try, our voices will inevitably betray us. Emotions affect voice speed, pitch, loudness, and timbre. Sure, we can control those aspects to a certain degree, but we're still better off simply learning techniques for not letting people push our hot buttons in the first place. Managing emotional states, ours and our customers', is a critical element in conflict resolution. When you think about it, there is no way you can effectively resolve conflict when your caller is at a heightened emotional state. Nor is it realistic to expect to resolve conflict when you are at a heightened emotional state. The greater the emotional stakes for you or your caller, the greater the chance that conflict will turn into confrontation. It makes sense, therefore, that your first step in resolving conflict is to prevent or reduce any associated negative emotions.

Each of us has our own positive and negative hot buttons, just as our callers do, and sometimes all it takes is for one disgruntled caller to start pushing them and ruin our whole day. To learn how to manage our emotions, we need to know what our own hot buttons are and learn to recognize when they're being pushed.

Your Hot Buttons

So what are your hot buttons? Think about the last few times you got upset. What were the situations? Hot buttons are interesting because it is typically the same emotional triggers each time. It could be criticism, a threat, a lack of respect, swearing, people who interrupt, sarcasm — any number of things. Although the situations in which you find yourself becoming emotional might change, the underlying triggers remain the same.

Take a moment and write down your hot buttons.

Beside them, write down why you think they bother you so much. Seriously, take the time to do this. It's a wonderful piece of self-analysis that has an instant impact on how those buttons affect you. I discovered several years ago, for example, that one of my hot buttons was when someone would question my credibility. It was a little disconcerting when I first realized this, and I felt a little silly about it. But after much introspection, I finally realized *why* this was an issue for me.

I'm the youngest of four boys by a wide margin, my brother closest in age to me being eight years my senior. As I think about it, I realize that from their perspectives I probably didn't have much valuable to add to a conversation until I was well into my 30s. I suspect that much of what I said for the first couple of decades of my life was pretty much ignored or dismissed. None of my brothers would have done this intentionally or to be hurtful, of course. Nor do I recall being either consciously aware of or upset by my not being taken seriously. I can understand now, however, why I used to crave credibility so much and why it became such a hot button for me.

The interesting thing is that, as soon as I began to identify the possible cause of this hot button, it started to lose its effect on me. I'd find myself starting to get upset, then instantly find myself thinking "Aha! I know why this is bothering me!" The negative emotion would quickly pass as I realized how silly its roots were. I've since learned that this is true of all hot buttons. So take the time to understand yourself better — the things that drive you and make you tick. This endeavor alone will help you to better manage your emotional states.

The next step, after learning to recognize what your hot buttons are and why they exist, is learning to recognize when they're being pushed. What are the initial signs that someone has triggered an emotional response in you? Unless we're paying close attention to the early signs, we usually don't recognize that we're becoming emotional until it's too late and the confrontation has already begun.

Our emotional states, for the most part, follow *patterned behavior.* Someone pushes one of our hot buttons, and, like a needle falling on a record, the same old song begins. Remember how your mom or dad had favorite lectures about certain subjects and you could almost recite them word for word? That's the kind of song I'm talking about. Emotional states are also progressive. The hot button gets pushed, the needle falls on the "That Irritates Me" track, and the emotional song starts to build. The song is fueled by our racing thoughts, our past experiences, and our caller, whose emotions are already dancing to their own tunes. Once you are in full flight, it is very difficult — if not impossible — to get the song out of your head. The secret is to stop the needle as soon as it hits the record.

The symptoms of someone pushing our hot buttons can vary, but here are the most common.

- Your heart starts to race.
- Your face turns red.
- You feel "tingly."
- Your head feels warm.
- Your breath is faster and shallower.
- Your jaw clenches.

Sound familiar? They are all symptoms of your autonomic physiological "fight or flight" mechanisms kicking in. And while you can't really control the adrenaline that's being generated, you can stop it before it becomes unmanageable.

Let's go back to the metaphor of a needle falling on a record. What would happen if you were to take a sharp object and scratch the record? The song, of course, would start to skip and never play the same way again. The secret to effectively managing the emotions that your hot buttons create is based on the same principle. You need to scratch your mental record. You need to use what is called a "pattern interrupter."

Pattern Interrupters

As the name suggests, pattern interrupters are things that alter your patterned behavior and sharply redirect your focus. There are a number of tremendously effective pattern interruption techniques. They fall into two basic categories: Redefining and Distorting.

Redefining is the process of attaching a different meaning to an action so that it doesn't push a hot button. For example, if people using profanity is a trigger, you can redefine how you view them by learning to think of them as unfortunate individuals with a limited command of the language. Rather than become defensive when someone speaks loudly, you can feel sorry for his lack of awareness.

Distorting is the process of removing the meaning from your trigger. It's the most common form of pattern interrupter and generally the most effective. Ever see the old movies in which someone slaps a hysterical person in the face, who in turn responds with shock and a "Thanks, I needed that"? That's a pattern interrupter. (Special note: no, I am *not* suggesting that you slap your callers!) The "slap in the face" routine instantly changes the other person's focus from the issue to the stinging cheek. The brain has to completely shift gears and address the question "What do I do now?"

Another well-known pattern interrupter is the

"picture everybody in their underwear" technique for overcoming the fear of public speaking. It's an effective way of briefly shifting your mental focus from your own insecurities outward to the audience. For those people who can easily visualize such things, it's a great technique. Another method, the "keyword" method, was explained to me by a CEO I met at a large conference. He had to get up in front of the audience of 1,000 or so people, give a five-minute "state of the nation" address, then introduce me as the keynote speaker. He was painfully uncomfortable in front of such a large group, but, because of his position and the number of addresses he gave every year, he'd been forced to learn how to deal with it. He used a word — one that he remembered from childhood — that always made him smile. Just as soon as he was introduced, he turned to me with a big smile and, in a Gomer Pyle throaty voice, said "Shazaam!" and then bounded onto the stage. His speech was fabulous.

Fortunately, interrupting your emotional pattern is much easier when you're on the telephone than when in person. You have the advantage of being able to do things that can't be seen by your caller. I mentioned earlier how my company sometimes wallpapers people's offices with specific images to achieve different emotional states. One of the most effective ways to interrupt your pattern when dealing with a caller works on the same principle.

Here's what you have to do. Some night when you're bored and sitting in front of the television, find a blank sheet of paper, steal some crayons from your child, and draw a picture of the Caller from Hell. Make the nastiest, silliest, goofiest-looking caller you can possibly imagine. Give him orange hair, fangs, and green teeth with stuff dripping from them. Use your imagination and have some fun with the picture. If you don't think you're imaginative enough, or have some crayon phobia, ask someone else to do it for you. If you have no friends and no family, you can cut out a horrible but funny picture from a magazine. If you're really stuck, go to my company's website and download an official Caller from Hell picture at www.beldingskills.com/cfh-picture.htm.

Keep the picture at your desk, where you can access it easily. As soon as you realize that you have a Caller from Hell on the other end of the line — as soon as you feel your hot buttons being pushed — put the picture in front of you and imagine that this is whom you're speaking with. You'll be amazed at how it changes your emotional state. Those physiological symptoms we discussed earlier will begin to dissipate, and you'll find yourself thinking about the situation much more clearly. Not convinced? Sounds too simple? Try it — you'll be surprised at how well it works!

The point of the exercise, of course, is not to trivialize or make light of the caller. It's simply a strategy for scrambling your patterned emotions long enough for your brain to have an opportunity to kick in. Once your intellect is in charge, instead of your emotions, your potential for a successful interaction improves dramatically.

The process of interrupting patterns might appear a little silly at first, maybe even unnecessary. Silly I can agree with, but they are certainly not unnecessary. You see, while conflict is an inevitable component in dealing with large numbers of people, confrontation is not. Confrontation is wholly preventable, and the prevention begins when we effectively manage our emotional states. The fact that many of the pattern-interrupting techniques you may hear about might be classified as "silly" is no accident. Remember that the purpose of the pattern interrupter is to jar us out of patterned behavior we have developed over a lifetime. To be effective, pattern interrupters have to create sharp contrasts to your existing way of thinking. "Silly" is one of the more effective ways of doing this. If you can't bring yourself to do this, if you are simply above such silliness, yet want the same results, I suppose you could try electric shocks to interrupt the pattern. But then you'd be faced with the task of having to explain your intermittent screams to your callers and coworkers.

PART TWO

A HOPE IN HELL

But on mine ears there smote a lamentation,
Whence forward I intent unbar mine eyes.

— DANTE'S *INFERNO*

CHAPTER SEVEN

LIFT THE RECEIVER

The message "I care" cannot be sent too often.

Okay, so we're all set. You've created the ideal environment. You're in a great mood. You're a role model for world-class telephone etiquette. Yet there he is — that Caller from Hell screaming into the earpiece. Now what?

Basically, Callers from Hell fall into two categories: unsatisfied callers and unreasonable callers. Unsatisfied callers represent the vast majority of Callers from Hell. These are people who had a certain set of expectations for you or your company that you failed to live up to. (Or, in some cases, they had negative expectations for you and your company that you succeeded in living up to.) As we discussed in chapter one, these are the callers with some combination of negative needs, personal situations, circumstances, personalities, or predispositions. While they may be *behaving* unreasonably, they aren't necessarily unreasonable people. It is on these unsatisfied callers whom we will focus the most.

Unreasonable callers, albeit often the most traumatic of callers, represent a very small group of people. They have unreasonable needs, make genuinely unreasonable demands, and have unreasonable expectations of you and your company. Because they tend to be unique in their unreasonableness, there is no universal strategy for dealing with them. We'll deal with them in section three of the book, "Calls of the Wild," one headache at a time.

When it comes to dealing with unsatisfied callers, however, there is a simple four-part process that works remarkably well almost all of the time. It's easy to remember — just think about it when you LIFT the receiver. LIFT is an acronym for the four key things we should have in mind every time we answer the telephone. These four things can help you win over the most unsatisfied of customers. The concepts aren't new. Nor are they difficult to understand. You just have to learn to execute them properly and consistently, and you will start to see success. Here are the four steps.

- **L**isten to your caller.
- **I**nvolve yourself.
- **F**ocus on the issues.
- **T**hank your caller.

Over the next four chapters, we will take a look at each element and how to execute it properly. You'll find that, as you practice the skills, they apply not just to Callers from Hell but to every person you talk with on the telephone.

CHAPTER EIGHT

LISTEN TO YOUR CALLER

If you begin at mediocre, by the end of the day there is no way you will be able to function at an acceptable level.

I suspect it comes as no surprise that the first and most important step in dealing with a difficult caller is to listen. Most of us have had the importance of listening drilled into our heads from a very young age — from our parents, our teachers, our coaches — even our spouses. But despite all of the reinforcement about the importance of listening, most of us are still only average listeners at best.

Have you ever found yourself becoming distracted in the middle of a conversation and then discovering to your dismay that you simply haven't heard large chunks of what the other person was saying? Have you ever had someone say to you "That's not what I said" or "I just said that"? I'd hazard a guess that you, like most of us, have. None of these things is an indicator of high-level listening skills.

Part of the challenge of listening is that, because most of us can hear, and have the innate capacity to listen at some level, we tend to take it for granted. We accept our listening abilities as they are and don't think much about developing them. The fact is, though, that truly effective listening — or "level one" listening, as the experts call it — is a skill that is as challenging to master as it is invaluable to attain.

In my job, I have the great pleasure of meeting a number of people who have excelled in the business world. I can state without hesitation that one of the most notable common denominators with all of the presidents, CEOs, and COOs I have met are their superior listening skills. The same skill is also evident with highly successful salespeople, health care providers, customer service representatives, and teachers. And whenever I'm introduced to people considered to be the superstars at resolving conflict in a company, listening is inevitably their most prominent trait.

So why is listening important? I mean, we've all been told that listening is important many times, but why? In the case of Callers from Hell, listening accomplishes two things. First, the more you listen, the more information you gather about the real issue. You get clues as to your caller's needs, situation, circumstance, personality, and predispositions. And with any luck, you develop a better understanding of why your caller is behaving the way he is.

People often suggest that the most common mistake we make when dealing with conflict is to become defensive. I'm not so sure about that. While becoming defensive is unquestionably a common result of feeling attacked, and a common mistake when we're in conflict, I believe there is another trap that we fall into in conflict situations that is far more devastating: *we try to resolve issues before we really understand what the issues are.* If I had to guess, I'd say that somewhere close to 90% of people, when dealing with a Caller from Hell, jump in with solutions before they really have adequate knowledge of the caller and her expectations. The end result, of course, is an escalation of conflict, because the caller now believes that you weren't listening to her. (And she'd be right!)

To illustrate, following is a call I once had the (pleasure?) of listening to. I've edited it a little to preserve the CSR's anonymity, but this is pretty much how it went. See if you can detect any resemblance to Abbott and Costello's famous "Who's on first?" routine.

Caller:	I bought two things last week but only received one.
CSR:	What is your order number?
Caller:	1234.
CSR:	It's showing here that you bought two things.
Caller:	Right, but I received only one.
CSR:	Which one didn't you receive?
Caller:	The blue one.
CSR:	Let me check on the status of it. . . .

Caller: Actually, since it didn't come, I went out and bought it elsewhere – so I would like a refund instead.

CSR: It should be there within a week.

Caller: But I don't need it now.

CSR: You want to cancel the order?

Caller: Right.

CSR: We can't cancel the order. You've already been shipped.

Caller: The blue one has already been shipped?

CSR: No, the red one has been shipped.

Caller: That's OK, I wanted the red one.

CSR: So you don't want to cancel the order?

Caller: I want to cancel the blue one.

CSR: It should be ready in a week.

Caller: But I've already purchased it!

CSR: I understand, sir, and it should be there within the week.

Caller: No – I've already purchased it somewhere else.

CSR: No, you bought it here, sir. It's on the purchase order.

Caller: I know, but I don't need it anymore.

CSR: So you want to cancel the order. . . ?

The customer, as you might expect, was quite upset by the end of the exchange. When the CSR was off the line with him, she turned to me and said, "I get crazy callers like this all the time — what do I do with them?" She was absolutely oblivious to her role in the exchange. She had no clue that, had she actually listened to her caller, she could have prevented a hostile exchange as well as reduced the length of the call from five minutes to one or two.

The second purpose of listening has to do with your caller's state of mind. You see, despite their differences, there is one thing that all of your Callers from Hell share. One common belief about you and your business. They think you don't care. It sounds a little harsh, but it's true. After all, if they had positive thoughts about you, why would they behave so badly? Imagine, for example, if you were calling and a close friend answered the phone. Would you still yell at him, or scold him, or act unreasonably? Probably not. You'd behave a little more civilly because, whatever the situation, you know that your friend is on your side. We need to send that same message to our callers.

Listening to someone — really listening to him — sends the message to your caller that he is important to you and that you're actually interested in what he has to say. And when you send this message, you create the foundation for helping your caller begin to manage his emotional state. If the caller was spoiling for a fight, he gets the message that he won't be having the fight with you. The more he talks, and the more you listen, the more time he has to vent his emotions. The more he has the opportunity to vent, the greater his control over his emotional state. The greater this control, the closer you get to resolving the conflict. I have never heard of a caller becoming upset because someone was listening too much.

Superior listening skills don't happen by accident. They're not something genetic that we either have or don't have. Attaining a higher level of listening skills is a product of a tremendous amount of practice and a focus on three key elements: undivided attention, prompting, and echoing.

1. Undivided Attention

Unless you're making notes that are in direct reference to what the customer is talking about (we'll talk more about that in just a moment), you should be doing nothing other than listening. Not doodling, not looking at unrelated e-mail on your computer screen, not rearranging your pencil drawer. Despite what we want to believe, our brains are not nearly as multitasking as we would like. Remember all that schoolwork you used to do in front of the television? You weren't actually doing two things at once. Your brain was shifting attention back and forth from one to the other. At best, you were simply dividing your time 50-50.

How long can you give someone your undivided attention? It's harder than you think. Not convinced? Try this exercise. The next time you answer the phone, begin timing yourself to see how long it takes before the first thought unrelated to the conversation enters your head. How long do you suppose you'll last before your thoughts stray to that unfinished report on your desk, what you should wear on your date Friday night, or how long until lunch? I can guarantee that, unless you're a trained listener, you'll be lucky to last 10 full seconds. And if you're like most people, not 15 seconds will pass before you've begun to divide your attention between what the caller is saying and formulating your response in your head.

Unfortunately, when it comes right down to it, most of us are pretty horrible when it comes to giving people our undivided attention. And even the experts — people who listen for a living — will tell you that they can give somebody their undivided attention for no more than five minutes at a time. High levels of listening require not only great skills but also much energy. Actually listening to and capturing all of the information and emotion someone is giving you can be quite exhausting. The technical term is "listener fatigue."

Listener Fatigue

Listener fatigue is the point where we have expended so much energy and focus in listening that our brains simply cease to process information as quickly or efficiently. It's a very real phenomenon, and it is important to be aware of. Telephone crisis intervention people will tell you that taking a serious call can be as draining as running a marathon. If they receive two serious calls in a row, the fatigue can jeopardize their ability to do their job effectively.

I have firsthand experience with listener fatigue. As you might imagine, I get to do a lot of traveling, with my training and speaking engagements taking me all over the world. In many of the countries I get to visit, English is a second, third, or fourth language for the people I meet. My seminars and speeches are, of course, delivered in English, and my clients and program participants are always kind enough to converse with me in my native language.

Understandably, many of the people who speak to me have fairly heavy accents and will occasionally use wrong words or awkward grammar structure. To converse with them, or to follow a heavily accented conversation, therefore, I have to give 100% of my concentration. I find that my need to concentrate is particularly necessary in Asian countries. Their native languages have significantly different cadences, inflections, and grammar structures, and these differences transfer to their English pronunciations. It usually takes me several days to become acclimatized to the way people speak. Wherever I am, though, by the time I get to the end of my first day, I find that my comprehension is significantly less than it was at the beginning of the day. I'm exhausted, and my brain hurts.

In a call center environment, awareness of listener fatigue is even more critical because listening is the only way you have to gather information about your customer. You can't count on picking up visual or kinesthetic clues, and when you start missing key details because of listener fatigue it can begin to create challenges.

Regardless of how much experience you have, listener fatigue is a fact of life. But here's the payoff to improving your listening skills: if you begin your day functioning at a high level of listening, listener fatigue might drop you down to mediocre by the end of the day or the end of your shift. Without the training, however, you're beginning at mediocre. And if you begin at mediocre, by the end of the day there is no way you will be able to function at an acceptable level.

Prompting

The second principle of effective listening on the telephone is prompting. This is the technique we use to encourage people to continue talking. And even though the things they say can sometimes be pretty nasty, we want our callers to talk. The more information we get, the easier it will be to resolve the issue; and the more the caller talks, the more likely her emotional state will begin to wind down.

Prompting is using single words or brief phrases that express empathy and interest and encourage the caller to talk more. When you prompt effectively, people reiterate points, clarify issues, and provide you with more details. Some familiar prompts are "Really?" "Is that right?" "Are you serious?" "Oh, no!"

Most of us instinctively prompt people when we're in a social environment — in situations where the conversations are pleasant. In the more unpleasant interactions with Callers from Hell, however, our prompting is typically replaced with grunting — "Mm-hm," "Uh-huh," et cetera. Don't grunt at your callers. Grunting is a bad thing.

Prompting is a useful skill to develop and has applications in all aspects of life. The next time you are having a discussion with your spouse, child, or coworker, practice it and observe how they respond. See how much information you can get out of them with simple words and phrases such as "Oh!" and "Really!" and "Is that right?"

What makes prompting so difficult when dealing with Callers from Hell is that it goes against our instincts. Our first instinct is to try to *remove* ourselves from the situation as quickly as possible, not to *encourage* someone's unpleasant behavior. The importance of having our callers keep talking to us can't be understated, however. It can be the difference between happy and grouchy moods for your callers and good and bad days for you.

Echoing

Have you ever been in an argument with someone only to find yourself repeating the things you've said, a little louder each time? We reiterate, reemphasize, and try to drive our message home. We're convinced that the other person "just doesn't get it" and that the only way to solve the problem is by increasing the frequency and volume of the message. Unfortunately, with every repetition, and every increase in volume, people's emotions increase proportionately. Because of this, it's essential that we communicate loudly and clearly to our callers that we do hear them and do, in fact, "get it." That's what echoing is all about.

Echoing, or "reflective listening," is the process of feeding back to your caller the real issues as he perceives them. It involves two steps. The first is learning to identify the real issues, and the second is repeating those issues back to your caller, as closely to word for word as possible.

The first part, identifying the issues, isn't as easy as it may first appear. Your caller will say many things over the course of your conversation. Some will be expressions of frustration, some will be hints as to what the caller is looking for, and some will be clues as to what the issue really is. Here are a few simple examples. See if you can pick the issues out.

1. The last person I talked to got my order wrong. Totally wrong. Don't any of you people know what the heck you're doing? Has your company ever thought of training you people? I hate calling this company. This is the worst experience I've ever had in my life!

2. Listen. You have a problem with this product. I have had these symptoms ever since I started taking it, and no one seems prepared to take responsibility! Believe me when I tell you, I'm going to take this right to the top if I have to. I recognize a cover-up when I see one!

3. I just went on-line and found out that I could have got this product for $300 less than you sold it to me for. What, do you think I'm stupid? I can't believe you ripped me off so much! And don't try to deny it — I recognize a scam when I see one!

In the first example, the issue statement is "The last person I talked to got my order wrong." The way to echo it is simple: "The last person you talked to got the order wrong?" The response from the caller will be "Yes!" and the subconscious message he gets will be "She understands." What about the other things the caller says in the first example? "I hate calling this company. This is the worst experience I've ever had in my life!" These are expressions of emotion. They're your caller's way of letting you know how frustrated or angry he is. Similarly, when he asks questions such as "Has your company ever thought of training you people?" chances are he isn't looking for an answer or a debate.

In the second example, the issue statement is "I've had these symptoms ever since I started taking it." The fact that "no one seems prepared to take responsibility" is the source of her frustration and her way of telling you that no one is acknowledging her discomfort. When she says things such as "Believe me when I tell you, I'm going to take this right to the top if I have to. I recognize a cover-up when I see one!" she is expressing her determination to have the issue resolved. The proper way to echo it is simply to say "You've had these symptoms since you started taking it?"

The best way to echo the third example is to say "You found it for $300 less somewhere else?" Again, when the caller refers to "scam" and "rip-off," he is simply expressing his frustration. If you were to respond to these statements, you'd only escalate the conflict. Your best bet is to ignore them.

Seem easy? Whenever we use examples like these in our workshops, and have people role-play these scenarios, over half of the group inevitably forget all about echoing and move straight to trying to resolve the issue. In the first example, for instance, most people respond with "What was your order supposed to be?" While this is a valuable question, it is not echoing and begs the caller to repeat himself. It's a classic example of our tendency to want to move toward a solution before ensuring we know what the issue really is.

One of the challenges with echoing is that, unlike in the examples above, your difficult caller may actually have talked for several minutes — which makes identifying that core issue statement very difficult. Listening with undivided attention is key. Another challenge has to do with voice tone. As we discussed in chapter three, the way you say things can make a dramatic difference in the message you send. Nowhere is this more important than in echoing. Use the wrong tone of voice, and you could easily come across as mocking or condescending, which, as you might expect, would only make things much worse.

Echoing is an incredibly valuable skill and has a remarkable effect on your caller's emotional state when done properly. The hardest part is to resist the temptation to jump in with questions or solutions. Remember, this is part of the *listening* process.

The Conflict Grid

One of the wonderful advantages of dealing with conflict over the telephone is that you can take notes and record your thoughts as they come to you. The benefits of this are huge. In most conflicts, when the other person is standing in front of you, you have to rely on your memory to capture and retain vital pieces of information. Unfortunately, the other person will often be communicating a lot of information to you, and by the time she's finished it's very easy for you to have forgotten one or two key elements. Not capturing this information can haunt you later when you're making decisions and your customer says to you "I've already told you that!" or "Weren't you listening?"

A couple of years ago I encountered a delightful woman named Ingrid, with 15 years of experience working in a large call center for a pharmaceutical company. Ingrid had devised a wonderful note-taking system to help her more effectively deal with unsatisfied customers. It worked so well in fact that, with her permission, we've incorporated it into many of our call center training programs.

If you take a look at the illustration on the next page, you'll see a page divided into four quadrants. In the upper left quadrant is "Issues & Information." In the upper right quadrant is "Emotion & Attitude." In the lower left quadrant is "Historical Information." And in the lower right quadrant is "Possible Solutions." Here's how it works. As the customer begins to talk, the things he is telling you usually begin to fall into one of three categories — what the issue is, how he feels about it, and what, if any, historical baggage he may be carrying with him. As the customer is speaking, you record what he says on the page — putting each sentence or thought into the appropriate quadrant.

SITUATION INFORMATION SHEET

ISSUES & INFORMATION	EMOTION & ATTITUDE
HISTORICAL INFORMATION	POSSIBLE SOLUTIONS

Here's an example of how it might work using an actual (abbreviated) transcript of a call that came into a travel agency. The caller was the husband and father of a family of four that was just beginning their vacation in the Caribbean. He was calling from the hotel.

Caller: Hi, it's John Smith calling. Have you actually been to this island before?

Agent: Yes, but I haven't actually been to the hotel you're at. Is there some sort of problem?

Caller: *[Sarcastically]* No. No problems at all! I mean, aside from the fact that my daughter has the flu, the airline has sent my luggage God knows where, and our hotel room is disgusting.

Agent: Oh, no.

Caller: Oh, yes. We asked for a room with two double beds, and we got a room with a queen-sized bed and a cot. The room wasn't made up when we got here, and whoever had been here before had been smoking in it. And I think you'll remember that I told you that my wife is desperately allergic to cigarette smoke. The airline told us that we were not going to see our luggage for at least another day. This is just a complete disaster. It's ruined. This trip cost us $6,000, and what are we getting for it? Nothing! Grief!

Now, I know what you're going to say – the same thing the travel agent said the last time something went wrong during a vacation – that it's out of your control. But you know what? I think it was at least your responsibility to have done your research to make sure we were flying on an airline that wouldn't lose our luggage and staying at a hotel that would give us a decent room. . . .

Here's what the call would look like when mapped out on the grid.

SITUATION INFORMATION SHEET

ISSUES & INFORMATION	EMOTION & ATTITUDE
• Daughter has flu.	• It's a disaster.
• Airline lost luggage.	• Vacation is ruined.
• Hotel is disgusting.	• Got nothing for $6,000.
• Queen size & cot instead of two doubles.	• Thinks I should have done better research on hotel & airline.
• Room not made up when arrived.	
• Cigarette smoke in room – Mrs. Smith allergic.	
• Luggage not coming for another day.	
HISTORICAL INFORMATION	**POSSIBLE SOLUTIONS**
• Travel agent on previous trip didn't help.	• Hotel comp room? Meals?
	• Airline comp?
	• Source doctor for daughter.

The great thing about this grid is that in a glance you can identify what the issues are, what the customer's mood is, and what kind of baggage (no pun intended) the caller is carrying with him; you can also jot down thoughts as they come to you without the risk of forgetting them. Once you become proficient with the grid, you can actually begin to track where you are in the conflict resolution process. As you continue to write, you can track the changes in the person's emotional state and how receptive the caller is to your ideas.

One of the pleasant side effects of writing in this grid while listening to someone is that the process of writing and dissecting the information forces you to keep focused on the issues and allows you to be a little more objective in how you deal with the situation. The caller's unpleasant behavior and heightened emotional state have less of a negative impact on you.

Here, again, are the keys to listening.

1. Give your caller undivided attention.
2. Prompt the caller for more information.
3. Echo the issue back to your caller.

Listening is often referred to as a "dynamic skill." There are no absolutes. You can't completely "master" it, because there is always room for improvement. No matter how good you are, or how good you think you are, it never hurts to practice and to find new tools to improve your effectiveness. It's really worthwhile. The payoff is immediate and significant.

CHAPTER NINE

INVOLVE YOURSELF

For many of your Callers from Hell,
a heartfelt apology is all they're looking for.

The cellular telephone company CSR broke the bad news. The caller hadn't passed the company's rigorous credit check and would have to provide a sizable deposit before the caller could have her phone activated. "We don't have that kind of money," the caller began to sob. And then the floodgates opened. "I know our credit is bad. We should have gone into bankruptcy when we lost our store five years ago, but we didn't. I know we're late in paying people, but we've had a lot of rough times. My son has already had three operations, and it's all we can do to stay ahead of the medical bills. We're self-employed and don't have medical insurance. . . ."

"Uh-huh," the bored CSR responded.

The next call was from a customer who was looking at adding two new phones to his existing account. "I'm getting married next week, and these are for my fiancée and daughter to be," he said excitedly.

"Uh-huh," the CSR responded again.

On the third call, the caller was upset that the company

had failed to credit him with a $150 rebate. It was the third time he'd called, and the situation still hadn't been fixed.

"Uh-huh," the CSR said as he scrolled through screens looking for the rebate information.

"Uh-huh?" the customer said incredulously. "That's all you have to say is 'uh-huh'? I've been a customer of this company for over 10 years, my company has 20 phones with you, and you're screwing me around for a crummy $150? I'll tell you what. I'll show you 'uh-huh.' I want you to cancel all of our accounts as of the end of the month. I'm sure that we can find another company that cares about our business!"

The CSR turned and looked at me with a baffled expression. He had no idea what had just happened or why. He'd fallen into the trap that so many people in the customer service industry get caught in. He'd heard the same stories so many times that he'd become numb. Callers had ceased to be living, breathing people and had become account numbers and open tickets. There's no faster way to create grouchy customers or to ensure that grouchy customers become even grouchier.

Listening, the first part of LIFT, is a tremendously valuable skill to develop regardless of what you do for a living. The effectiveness of listening in helping people to manage their emotional states is almost completely negated, however, when the customer gets the impression that you just don't care.

By listening, you begin to break down some of the perceived barriers between you and the caller. Instead of getting the fight or the hassle he was expecting, your caller has got a willing ear. After only a couple minutes of patient listening, you can start to hear the edge come off the caller's voice. You may still be in conflict, but you are less and less in confrontation. To continue this process, it's critical that you learn how to *involve* and *engage* yourself with your caller. You need to build rapport and trust; you need to show interest and respect. In the world of negotiating, it is referred to as "stepping to their side" — the point where your caller still has an issue to resolve but perceives you as an ally instead of an adversary.

Involving yourself means communicating to your caller that you care and that you genuinely want to become involved in helping him find a solution. You have to let him know that you understand the situation and empathize with what he's going through. Involving yourself does not necessarily mean *agreeing* with his point of view, but it does mean acknowledging that you understand how he feels and that you don't want him to be unhappy. In the Five Cs of Influence, it is compassion.

In the example above, the CSR comprehended his callers' issues and was both competent and confident. He definitely lacked cheerfulness, and if he had any compassion whatsoever he certainly didn't communicate it well. His inability or unwillingness to display compassion eventually, in the third call, compromised his ability to do his job. And although we have no way of knowing for sure, there is also a real possibility that his attitude could have resulted in unseen consequences in the first two calls as well. Remember that, on average, we tell 10 people about a poor service encounter. Do you suppose that the first two callers may have told some people about their unpleasant experiences?

A great comparison of the importance of communicating your compassion can be found in the medical profession. We refer to it as "bedside manner." A 2004 Harris Interactive poll of over 2,000 respondents found that people cared more about doctors being compassionate than they did about doctors being up to date on the latest medical research and treatment. An examination of 25 individual studies on doctor-patient relationships consistently found that doctors with good bedside manners had a better impact than physicians who were less personal.

Expressing compassion — involving yourself — doesn't require you to go out and buy sympathy cards or invite people over to your house. It requires only that you reflect back the appropriate emotion to your caller. You do so through your tone of voice and the words you choose. If something positive has happened, as in the second example above, all the CSR needs to say to involve himself is "You're getting married — congratulations!"

When it comes to Callers from Hell and potential Callers from Hell, as in the first and third examples, the best language anyone can use is "I can understand why you're frustrated." These six words are invaluable in involving yourself with your caller ("frustrated" can be replaced with whatever the appropriate emotion might be — "angry," "upset," "frightened," etc.). In expressing yourself this way, you are conveying to your caller that you understand his emotions. You aren't necessarily agreeing with his position or opinion, but you are recognizing his emotional state and his right to feel that way.

Part of creating this bond of empathy with your caller is not to be afraid to apologize when you or someone else in your company has done something wrong. This, I recognize, runs somewhat contrary to today's popular school of thought, which can best be characterized by the political saw "deny, deny, deny." In today's unfortunate, hyper-litigious atmosphere, it's all too easy to fall into a butt-covering "admit nothing, apologize for nothing," routine. And while it may protect you from the occasional hungry lawyer, I believe it is absolutely counterproductive when it comes to generating loyalty. For many of your Callers from Hell, a heartfelt apology is all they're looking for. Most of us can forgive someone who makes an honest mistake. When you appear to be unwilling to either recognize or acknowledge a mistake, however, it simply sends the message loudly and clearly that you don't care. Think of the third caller in the example above. Do you suppose his reaction might have been a little different if, instead of the CSR responding with "Uh-huh," he'd said, "Wow, I can understand why you'd be frustrated. I'm really sorry this has happened to you." I do. I think that, with those two simple sentences, the CSR would have saved his company many thousands of dollars.

Let's use that third caller to see how the whole call might have gone if the CSR had used the first two steps in LIFT.

Caller:	Hi. I'm hoping you can help me. I just got our most recent bill. I was expecting to see a $150 credit for a phone we purchased four months ago."
CSR:	*[Prompting]* Oh, really?
Caller:	Yes. They told me in the store that it was a rebate that was supposed to be applied to my next bill. Well, it's three bills later, and I've called three times, and I still have no credit. What's going on?
CSR:	*[Prompting]* Oh, no!
Caller:	Oh, yes! And I don't mind telling you that I'm starting to get a little frustrated!
CSR:	*[Echoing]* You've called three times, and you still haven't received your rebate?
Caller:	That's right. And if I have to call again, it will be to cancel our phones!

CSR: I would hate to see that! *[Involving himself]* But I sure can understand why you're frustrated! I'm really sorry this has happened to you.

Caller: Me too. I've really been satisfied with your company's service up until now. But my boss is all over me about controlling expenses, and this is just the type of thing he'll go nuts about.

CSR: *[Prompting]* Oh-oh. *[Involving himself]* I understand why you need this fixed!

Caller: And fast. . . .

Do you see the change in the customer's attitude? The problem's not solved yet, but the potential for confrontation has diminished greatly. We've learned that the real issue isn't as much the rebate as it is the caller's fear of repercussions from his boss. Simply by following the first two steps of LIFT the CSR's response would change. Maybe, for example, after he fixes the issue, he might volunteer to fax through a letter of confirmation to the caller — just so he has some paperwork to show his boss.

Although I present LIFT as a process, you can see that the components are ongoing. You may find yourself, for example, echoing several times or having to reaffirm your involvement more than once. The message "I care" cannot be sent too often.

CHAPTER TEN

FOCUS ON THE ISSUES

If you aren't able to maintain the focus of a call, it becomes very easy for your caller to get frustrated, believing that you just don't understand the problem.

The most important steps in dealing with Callers from Hell are the first two — listening and involving yourself. From experience, my guess would be that close to 60% of the difficult calls you encounter will result in a happy ending for everyone if you do nothing but master those two skills. The remaining 40%, however, require some additional effort and skill in keeping the conversation focused.

Many calls "go sideways" not just because of the listening skills of the CSR or a lack of desire to do a good job but because the issue is too complex or multi-tiered to be dealt with using traditional language strategies. Using the Situation Information Sheet introduced in chapter eight can help a lot in making sense of information in your own mind, but it's a different story entirely when you and a customer are trying to discuss complex details.

I experienced a great example of this with my company's cellular telephone provider several years ago. In

November, I received a call from a telephone sales rep. She told me that she had been reviewing our account and that, with a few modifications to our mobile plans, she could cut our monthly bill in half. All she had to do, she said, was change our status from a "small" company to a "medium" company. She would ship us an additional seven phones so that we would qualify for the change in plans. The phones would be free, as part of the new activation promotion, and somehow, magically, our bills would be dramatically reduced.

I mentioned to her that we had no use for an additional seven lines or phones; nor did we expect to need them in the near future. She explained that that didn't matter — but she would have to create seven new lines to give us the special rates. The whole thing sounded a little odd, to say the least. I told her that I wasn't prepared to make that kind of decision at the moment and asked her to call me back in January.

While I wasn't interested in the seven unnecessary phones, she had piqued my interest on another matter. She had in her analysis brought to my attention a number of billing errors that had been recurring for almost a year. I made a note of them and over the course of the next few weeks reviewed all of the bills to identify all of the irregularities; I discovered that we were due over $400 in credits for errors in the previous year. Finally, in December I called the company to have it corrected. The

CSR advised me that the credit would be applied on our January bill.

In the first week of January, much to my surprise, we received a shipment of seven phones, along with a packing slip, information about the phone number for each phone, and a contract to sign. In the second week of January, we received a 30-page bill. I was baffled. I called and left a message for the salesperson to call me to straighten things out. I put all of the phones and the unsigned contract in the corner of my office, then forgot about everything until the next month when the next bill arrived, this time showing "late payment" charges. To make matters worse, there was still no sign of the $400 credit we were to have received in January. I called and left another message. By the third month, still with no response, I gave up trying to contact the salesperson and called customer service to straighten things out. It was a nightmare.

The CSR with whom I spoke was quite nice but simply didn't have the skill to deal with this complex an issue. I compounded the challenge by telling her about the phone fiasco *and* the $400 credit. Big mistake. She couldn't get her head around these being two separate issues. It took over two months and half a dozen telephone conversations with as many different people in order for it to get resolved.

What made the situation so interesting was that the

actual solution was pretty straightforward. The company took the phones back, put us back on our original plan, credited us for the three months we were on the wrong plan, and credited us the $400. But it took six CSRs, and my explaining the situation six times, before we managed to get there. The difference between the first five CSRs and the one who finally resolved the issue was her skill in *focusing*. She did so by creating checkpoints along the way and using them as reference points to ensure that we didn't keep revisiting issues or getting one issue confused with the other. Here's how she did it.

She began beautifully. As you may expect, by this time I was a Very Unhappy Caller. She listened to what I had to say and responded with "Mr. Belding, I am so sorry. I don't understand how all of this happened to you, but I am not going to get off the phone until I've got everything fixed."

I responded dryly with "It's been six weeks so far — you might be in for a long night."

She replied by echoing "You've been trying to have this fixed for six weeks? This keeps getting worse!"

I knew I was going to like this woman.

"Mr. Belding," she said, "it seems like there are a lot of things going on here. If you can bear with me, I would like to deal with them one at a time — that way nothing will get forgotten."

I agreed.

"First of all, you've got $400 worth of billing adjustment we need to make from the previous year. Let's just refer to this from now on as 'the $400' so we don't get it confused with anything else." She listened patiently while I explained the details to her and then said, "Mr. Belding, you are absolutely right that we owe you a credit. I'm really sorry that your billing had these problems. And I'm not sure why it didn't happen the first time you called in. I am issuing the credit now, and it will appear on your next statement. Before we're done, I'm also going to give you all of my contact information so that if the credit doesn't appear — which it should — you can call me directly."

After a brief pause as she entered everything into her computer, she continued, "Now, let's talk about these additional seven lines and seven phones. You didn't want them in the first place, but they were shipped to you anyway?" After I filled her in, she continued with "Let's call this 'the seven phones' just so we don't confuse it with 'the $400' or the changes that have happened to your plan. I am going to cancel these numbers right now and make arrangements for us to pick the phones up from your office today or tomorrow. Mr. Belding, I don't understand why we sent you seven phones you don't need, but I do want to apologize for it. You must think we're just crazy."

And that is the way the call went for a little over an

hour. The CSR isolated an issue, gave it a name, apologized for it, and dealt with it. At the end, she recapped everything that had happened. "Mr. Belding, let me just recap what we've done, just so we can make sure that I haven't missed anything. I have seven issues that we dealt with.

1. The $400 – we've credited your account the amount from the billing errors.
2. The seven phones – we've canceled the seven phones, and Fedex will be at your office to pick them back up by tomorrow noon.
3. The 30-page bills – I have canceled the past three months' worth of bills. You can ignore the January to March statements you have – just throw them out.
4. The past due interest – I have credited your account for any past due charges for the past three months.
5. Old plan – I have reinstated your company on the plan you originally had before this whole mess began.
6. Rebilling – I have arranged for you to be rebilled for January to March based on the old plan.
7. Follow-up – I have made a note to contact you in one month, after you have received your latest bill, to ensure that everything is the way it should be."

By breaking the call down into seven distinct checkpoints, and naming the checkpoints to avoid confusion, the CSR was able to tackle the situation. She kept the call focused, kept me focused, and brought things to a clear resolution. Her recap of each checkpoint at the end confirmed that we'd dealt with everything, and it gave me the confidence that things were finally under control. At the end of the call, she said, "Mr. Belding, I can't apologize enough for the challenges you have faced. You are a very important customer, and this is not the way we like to do business. Thank you so much for sticking with us, and thank you for giving me the opportunity to correct things."

Wow.

Here are the four steps for maintaining focus in a complex call.

1. Create checkpoints by isolating each separate issue.
2. Give each checkpoint a name for easy reference.
3. Deal with each checkpoint before you move on.
4. Recap the checkpoints and the resolutions at the end.

It doesn't have to be a complex call for things to go sideways, of course. Sometimes our callers just have difficulty communicating and staying on topic. In those situations, your skill level in controlling a conversation through directed questioning is critical (see chapter five). It is also good to learn how to bring someone back to the issue gently so as not to offend her.

Let's say, for example, that someone calls in to

complain about late shipment on an order, then switches gears and begins to talk about how your competitor is selling its product for less. You could say, "Excuse me, yergunnahafta stay focused on one issue at a time," but you run the risk of offending your caller. What if, instead, you worded it so that you emphasized the benefits to the caller? For example, "Oh, no! Actually, if you don't mind, I'd like to sort out this late shipment issue for you before we move on to something else — I don't like having dissatisfied customers!"

If you aren't able to maintain the focus of a call, it becomes very easy for your caller to get frustrated, believing that you "just don't understand." It can also become very disconcerting and stressful for you when you find yourself attempting to come up with a solution to an unclear issue. It's like trying to hit a moving target. It's not always realistic to expect your customer to be able to focus on the issue. Her emotional state — frustration, anger, and so on — and lack of understanding of your company's processes make it very difficult for her to organize her thoughts in the best possible manner for achieving a solution. That's why it's important that you do it. Not only will you be able to resolve issues faster and more efficiently, but your caller will also perceive you as having greater competence and confidence.

CHAPTER ELEVEN

THANK YOUR CALLER

Although it's not a lot of fun to deal with a Caller from Hell, she is actually a tremendous asset to us. She is the one to inform us of the frustrations that 50 other customers are having but aren't bothering to tell us about.

You've listened to the caller, prompting her to give you as much information as she can. You've echoed the key issues and recorded everything for easy reference. You've involved yourself and expressed compassion. You've remained focused on the issue and dealt with things efficiently and effectively. Now, like the follow-through on a golf swing, it's time to end properly so that your caller's experience is as positive as possible throughout your interaction. Simply put, it's time to apply the finishing touches.

At the center of a call's finishing touches is the part where you thank your caller for the call. Without question, this can be the most important part of the process when it comes to turning Callers from Hell into callers who are both satisfied and loyal. I know that it might seem a little odd to say "Thank you" to someone who's been behaving rudely. It is, however, a very important step and one that is all too often missed.

Think about it for a moment. Do you think that most people, when dissatisfied with a product or service, will tell you about it? No. In fact, the research tells us that, out of every 100 poor service experiences our customers have, we only ever hear about two. Oh, sure, they'll tell lots of other people — at least 10 — but they don't tell us. This makes it pretty hard to learn from our mistakes.

So, although it's not a lot of fun to deal with a Caller from Hell, she is actually a tremendous asset to us. She is the one to inform us of the frustrations that 50 other customers are having but aren't bothering to tell us about. The other 50 callers? They did what most of us do — they simply hung up and never called back, perhaps to leave as customers forever. A sincere "Thank you for bringing this to our attention" is not only something your caller wants to hear but also a legitimate and genuine sentiment.

The other thing these Callers from Hell are doing that the other 50 aren't is giving you a second chance. They haven't "defected" or walked away forever just to tell all of their friends about their unpleasant experiences. They've given you an opportunity to correct the situations, so saying "Thank you for giving us the opportunity to correct this" is a most appropriate gesture.

In addition to thanking your caller, there are a few other finishing touches that can help to ensure you leave the call on the best note possible.

Ask What Else

Once you have completely resolved the issue, the next step is to ask if there is anything else that you can do for your caller. Even though you might feel that you can't wait to get off the phone with this person, you still need to ask the question. The purpose of saying "Is there anything else I can do for you today?" is twofold. First, now that you have built a degree of rapport with your caller, it's the ideal time to deal with any other issues that might be lurking in the background. Second, by offering to provide additional assistance, you reinforce to your caller that he is important and that you care that he is satisfied.

Restate Your Name

Usually, by the time you have resolved the issue, your caller has long since forgotten your name. In one sense, it's unfortunate because, if you've done a good job in building rapport and resolving the issue, your caller doesn't know whom to say nice things about. More importantly, though, by reminding the caller of your name, you're ending the call as a real, live person providing personal service.

Invite the Caller to Call Back

The final message you want to send to your caller is that he is welcome to call back. As with asking what else you can do for him, this message reaffirms your interest in his satisfaction.

Here's what the finishing touches might sound like.

CSR: Mr. Watson, thank you again for taking the time to call us. Is there anything else that I can do for you today?

Caller: No, I'm fine, thank you.

CSR: Great. Again, my name is Paul. If there is anything else you require, or if there is anything else we can do, please call any time.

CHAPTER TWELVE

SILENCE IS NOT GOLDEN

So, what are you going to do about it, bub?

In chapter two, we discussed the importance of reducing customer wait time. The truth is, though, that most of us have very little control over the staffing and system decisions that impact customer wait time. But we all have control over a different kind of wait time — whether we work in a call center or in an office. We have control over those periods of silence that we create *after* we have connected with a customer. I refer to it as *hold time*. Hold time is created when we say, "Would you please hold for a moment while I look into this?" Or those times when we don't actually put people on hold but work away on our computers in silence, scrolling through window after window, waiting for things to show up on the screen.

We have a wonderful exercise we conduct in our call center training programs to demonstrate the difference in time perceptions between the serviceperson who has put a person on hold and the person who has been put on hold. We separate the participants into two groups, then put each group in a separate room. I tell the people in the first room that I have to go to the other room and that I will be back shortly. I give them explicit instructions that they are not to speak to each other until I get back. I then go to the other room and give the participants there a questionnaire to fill out. I go back to the first room precisely one minute later and ask the group to write on a piece of paper how long they think I've been gone. I then return to the second room after exactly one minute and ask the group there to write down how long they think I've been gone.

Without fail, the group that has the task to do perceives the time as less than half as long as the group who is sitting in silence with nothing to do. The parallel to our interactions with callers is clear. When we put someone on hold to complete a task, we're *doing* something. We're talking to a team leader, we're looking at documents, and so on. Our callers, like the first group in my training sessions, are simply waiting for us to return. You can see how this waiting causes our callers to perceive time as moving much more slowly than we do. One airline call center regularly had customers complaining "I've been on hold for 20 minutes!" We knew, because of the telephone system, that it was actually closer to seven or eight minutes — but that's how the callers were perceiving it. I think we can all relate to this. We've all been put on hold and wondered if the person at the other end has gone on a coffee break or something. It's a horrible feeling, and, for a customer who already has a negative set of expectations, it just begins to increase her stress level.

I remember a wonderful experience with a Bell telephone customer service representative. I'd discovered to my horror that, for some reason, my company wasn't showing up in the 411 information directory. This meant that people would call directory information and ask about the company, but the operator would be unable to find it. It was a little frightening to think that, after more than a decade of being in business, I didn't exist.

The CSR I spoke with was delightful. You could feel her positive mood through the telephone as well as her concern and her grasp of the situation. She made a point to communicate her empathy and to keep things on the lighter side by saying things such as "Gee, I guess if you don't exist, I don't actually have to talk with you — but I will anyway, because you seem like a nice person."

And as she went through the steps to check into the matter, she talked me the entire way through it. "Just while I have you on the phone," she said, "let me check out the system to see if you show up. OK . . . let's see here . . . open this screen . . . Belding . . . 411 . . . move over to that screen . . . no, I don't need to know that . . . yes, there's the listing . . . and . . . well, look at that — you don't exist in this database! Let's take a look in the other database. Just a moment. OK . . . get rid of this screen . . .

open that screen . . . close this window . . . carry the one
. . . hold your partner, spin around, dosey-doe . . . here
we go . . . here's the screen . . . it's coming, and . . . no —
you don't exist here either. Now, are you sure you actually do exist?"

And so on it went, until finally she said, "I can't
explain it. Now, the next question is how do we fix it?
I've never encountered this before. . . ." She proceeded to
talk me through an entire process that she didn't need
me there for. She could have, as I believe most people
would have, just done this in silence, leaving me hanging, wondering what, if anything, she was doing. The
end result was that the time passed far more quickly for
me, and I ended up with a greater appreciation of her
efforts and what she'd done to resolve the situation.

On the telephone, silence is *not* golden. Whether it's
the silence that comes from being put on hold, or the
silence while you are doing a task, it creates discomfort
for your caller. There are two things you can do about
silence.

1. Set Expectations

Typically, when we put people on hold, we say things
such as "Can I put you on hold for a moment?" Asking

permission to put someone on hold is proper etiquette, and, as we discussed in chapter two, it's a good idea to tell people *why* you are putting them on hold. To prevent the caller from becoming annoyed at the perceived length of time she is put on hold, however, it's also a good idea to set expectations for her. So, instead of saying "May I put you on hold for a moment?" estimate how long you expect to be and tell her. For example, "May I put you on hold to talk with my supervisor for about three minutes?" Or "May I put you on hold to talk with my supervisor? It should take about three minutes." This approach gives your caller a frame of reference, and because of it she will typically be a little more patient.

If it looks like you'll be taking longer than you estimated, make sure that you get back on the phone to touch base with your caller. Let her know that you haven't abandoned her, and reestimate the time. For example, "Ms. Smith? My apologies for the delay. It looks like I might still be another two minutes. Is that all right?" If your company doesn't have a touch-base standard, then you should set one for yourself. A touch-base standard is the maximum length of time you will allow to pass before you get back on the telephone to touch base with your caller. I'd recommend no longer than 90 seconds as a rule of thumb.

2. Give Callers a Play-by-Play Account

Give your caller a play-by-play account of what you're doing and why you're doing it. It doesn't have to be as detailed or as chatty as my example of the telephone CSR, but you do want to keep your caller engaged throughout the call.

Silent Messages

There's another aspect of silence that you need to be aware of when dealing with any difficult person, whether over the telephone or in person. It's the silent messages that we can send when we don't control the call by asking questions of our callers (see chapter five). Let me give you some examples.

Several years ago I was trying to reserve a hotel room with a clerk who gave every indication of just not wanting me there. I asked her for a king-sized bed in a nonsmoking room with high-speed Internet access. There was a brief silence while she typed on her keyboard, and then she responded with "I'm sorry, we have none of those rooms available." I waited for her to tell me what was available, but I got only silence. I had a vivid picture in my head of her standing there with arms crossed and a smug look on her face, thinking to herself

"So, what are you going to do about it now, bub?"

I responded with "Do you have *any* rooms with high-speed Internet access available?"

"Yes," came the answer, followed by more silence (so, what are you going to do about it, bub?).

On another occasion, I was calling my company's bank, trying to set up a merchant credit card account. "Yergunnahafta have a security deposit in order to get one," the bank employee told me. Then a pause (so, what are you going to do about it, bub?).

Another example is when I had to take a VCR back to the store for repairs. It still had a valuable tape in it. "We can send it in to be fixed," the employee said coolly, "but you're not gunna get your tape back." This time I could actually see the crossed arms and the defiant look in her eyes. And while, like the others, she didn't actually say "So, what are you going to do about it, bub?" I heard it loud and clear in my head.

When you mention something to your caller, but don't give him a clue as to what the next step is, you abdicate control of the situation and make everyone uncomfortable. You put your caller in the awkward situation of having to take control — a position that he is neither qualified for nor comfortable with. In my example of the hotel reservation, I had no way of knowing what the stumbling block was. Was it the nonsmoking room? The king-sized bed? The high-speed

Internet access? In the case of the bank, I didn't know what the next steps were. And in the case of the broken VCR, I had no idea what my options were.

In each of these cases, my discomfort would have been overcome if the serviceperson had simply taken control and *asked a question.* Look at how differently the interactions might have gone if each person had followed the statements with questions.

Reservations clerk:	I'm sorry, we have none of those rooms available. How would a nonsmoking room with Internet access and two double beds be?
Bank employee:	Yergunnahafta have a security deposit in order to get one. Would you like some more information about it?
Store employee:	We can send it in to be fixed, but you're not gunna get your tape back. Do you want to try taking it to the repair place yourself and see if they can have it removed?

Can you see the difference a simple question makes and how much more comfortable it is than silence? By asking a question, the serviceperson provides direction to the customer, and the customer then has something concrete to respond to.

Silence over the telephone is deadly. It creates

discomfort and just begs to be misinterpreted. Remember, the one thing all your Callers from Hell have in common is that they think you don't care. The last thing you want to do is reinforce this message by asking your customer to interpret an awkward silence.

CHAPTER THIRTEEN

ACCENTS AND LANGUAGE BARRIERS

*What's important is that you continue to let her know
you care and that you want to work with her.*

The Ethnologue organization, one of the most recognized
authorities on languages, has classified 6,912 distinct
languages in the world. When you think about it, it's
pretty amazing that we can even communicate with
people from different cultures at all. Language barriers
are an inevitable part of life in our increasingly connected and ever-shrinking world. They create a number
of challenges and frustrations for everyone involved.
And when you remove the visual components — gestures,
body language, facial expressions, et cetera — these challenges are magnified greatly.

This challenge of language really sunk in for me the
first time I had the opportunity to work in Malaysia.
English, fortunately, is a common second language for
most Malays, but not everyone was fluent in it. While I
was at the hotel, things were pretty good — it was a
world-class hotel that catered a great deal to an English-
speaking clientele. When we left the capital city of Kuala
Lumpur, however, I found my ability to communicate a

little more restricted. The Malays I encountered, fortunately, lived up to the country's reputation as being warm and helpful, and I managed to get by by smiling a lot and using many hand gestures. My biggest test came, however, when I was using the telephone trying to make some arrangements with someone who seemed to be fluent in both Malay and Mandarin but not so much in English. Fortunately, she was extremely patient, because it took us almost half an hour to find enough words in common to get our respective messages across. I can't remember the last time I felt so helpless.

You should focus on two important areas when interacting with callers for whom your language is their second language: (1) how you deal with your own predispositions, and (2) how you deal with your caller.

How You Deal with Your Own Predispositions

Have you ever stopped to think about how accents impact how you feel about another person? The impact is likely much more significant than you think. Try as we might to ignore stereotypes and predispositions, they still exist in our minds and affect how we behave. Do you believe you are accent deaf? Imagine if you will the phone ringing in your house. You answer it, and it's someone you don't know. He's an investment broker claiming to have been referred by a mutual friend, and he'd like to drop by and introduce himself. The person could have one of, say, four accents: Southern U.S. English, Mandarin, Middle Eastern, or Spanish. Do you really believe that you'd give the credibility and trustworthiness of each caller equal weight?

There is a mountain of research demonstrating how accents color our actions and opinions. A study out of the University of North Texas, for example, showed that people with pronounced Texan accents stood a far greater chance of landing a job in Texas than people with other regional U.S. accents. Several other studies show that people speaking English with accents outside what is referred to as the "inner circle" (i.e., Great Britain, the United States, Canada, Australia, and New Zealand) are perceived as less credible and less competent teachers.

The point is, whether we like it or not, accents can color how we perceive people and ultimately how we treat them. To be effective at our jobs, we have to be aware of our preconceptions and learn to deal with them. It might help you to consider the fact that your accented caller speaks at least two languages — perhaps several. This fact alone deserves your respect.

How You Deal with Your Caller

You have a caller on the line with a heavy accent, and you are struggling to make out what she is saying. Are there any strategies you can use to improve your interaction? Absolutely. Remember that, if you think *you're* having a tough time, it's nothing compared with how your caller is feeling. She's likely feeling stressed, frustrated, and incompetent.

There are three things you have to do when communicating with someone who is struggling with the language. First, you have to reassure your caller that you respect her and empathize with her; second, you have to continually send the message that you will be patient and that you want to help; and third, you have to use all of your active listening skills to the best of your ability.

Begin by acknowledging the difficulty. It makes no sense to try to ignore the obvious challenge and even less sense to pretend that you understand her. Because she's already feeling a little insecure, try to shoulder the communication challenge yourself. So, instead of saying "Ms. Devine, your accent is hard to understand," try saying "I'm sorry, Ms. Devine, I'm having a little difficulty . . ."

Follow this statement by asking your caller if she'd mind slowing down her speech as much as she can. Explain that you want her to slow down so you will be able to help her better. And make sure that you *ask* her, not tell her. Here's an example.

Wrong way: Ms. Devine, your accent is hard to understand. Yergunnahafta speak slower.

Right way: I'm sorry, Ms. Devine, I'm having a little difficulty understanding. Could I ask you to speak a little slower so that I can make sure I can do the best job for you?

As she is speaking, listen carefully and make a point to confirm anything that you're unsure of. Don't worry about asking too many questions. Questions are good. What's important is that you continue to let her know that you care and want to work with her. Don't rush her, and don't express annoyance or impatience. Whenever possible, try to find something that the two of you can laugh at. Laughter is a wonderful equalizer.

One other thought. If you find that a large proportion of your callers have similar ethnic backgrounds, prepare yourself by writing down some key phrases in their language. How you pronounce the words is irrelevant. What is important is how much more comfortable your callers will feel when they hear you trying to connect with them.

These are some ideas for learning how to better understand your caller, but what can you do to make *yourself* a little better understood? Here are five simple tips.

1. Slow down. If the language you are speaking is not the caller's first language, chances are your caller is trying to translate what you are saying into her language as you speak. This means that you have to slow right down and speak in phrases. This does not mean, of course, speaking louder, as people often do.

2. Use the simplest words you can to express yourself. Complex, multi-syllabic words can intimidate and confuse your caller.

3. Repeat yourself. Try to express yourself in a few different ways. This gives your caller more than one opportunity to understand you. For example, "Mr. Stern, you should be able to find the product ID number on the bottom of the machine. If you turn the machine over so that it's upside-down, it should be right in front of you. Just flip it over in your lap."

4. Give your caller permission to stop you and ask questions if he doesn't understand what you are saying. You can say something like "If I go too fast for you, just let me know."

5. Ensure that you manage your tone of voice so that your caller doesn't perceive frustration from you. A neutral tone is best when speaking to someone in a language that might not be her first.

PART THREE

HOUNDS OF HELL

Let us descend now unto greater woe.

— DANTE'S *INFERNO*

CHAPTER FOURTEEN

CALLS OF THE WILD

Giving up is no substitute for being skilled.

Until now, we've focused on some of the things we can do to help create a world-class call center and minimize the number of Callers from Hell we encounter. We have looked at why callers become dissatisfied, at strategies for managing their emotional states, and at the LIFT process for converting Callers from Hell into loyal, satisfied customers.

For some callers you'll encounter, however, these strategies will have only limited effect. These are our unreasonable callers. People who have unreasonable expectations of us or our companies. People who present unique and stressful challenges. Fortunately, in the world of Callers from Hell, we don't encounter these types very often, but they are out there, and there are ways to deal with them.

I've heard some pretty strange calls over the years and could fill a book with accounts of some of the more crazy callers. I'll focus instead on the ones who seem to pop up most often. They're the ones you're most likely to encounter.

Unfocused

Roses are red,
Violets are blue,
I have a short attention span, and
Oh, look — there's a bus!

Some customers just seem to have a hard time staying on topic. They bounce from one issue to the next without even taking a breath. By the time they've talked for two or three minutes, you're so thoroughly confused that you don't even know where to begin. Here's an example of a call to a mutual fund company that I had the opportunity to listen to:

> Hi. I just wanted to find out how my mutual funds are doing. They're the ones that my advisor advised me to buy. I'm still not sure that he bought the right ones – the ones that I originally said that I wanted to get – because I didn't keep any notes on it, but I'm pretty sure that I wanted one of those ones with the ethical companies in it, but I guess it doesn't matter as long as I'm making money, right? But I'm just not quite sure how my mutual funds are doing. Actually, I'm not quite sure how my broker's doing – do you have any way of telling me if my broker is actually any good or not? This is my retirement, you know – even though I'm a long way from retirement, I want to make sure that I've got enough money. . . .

The temptation with a caller like this is to interrupt her in the middle of her chatter, back her up to the beginning, and get her to focus — just as we discussed in chapter ten. It won't work in this case. One of the biggest reasons your unfocused caller is behaving this way is because she has a lot on her mind. She herself feels overwhelmed and isn't sure how to organize her thoughts. She already feels a little insecure. If you cut her off, or if she perceives that you are treating her in a condescending manner, she'll just feel worse. The one thing you don't want to do is turn her insecurity into anger.

The first rule when dealing with the unfocused caller is patience. Just let her keep talking until you're pretty sure she's run out of things to say.

The second rule is to make sure you have a pen and a piece of paper in front of you. As the caller talks, *write everything down*. This will help you to remember details so that you can help put things in order for your caller. Whatever you do, don't just try to rely on your memory.

The third rule is to confirm your understanding of the issues your caller has brought up. So you might say something like this:

Thank you, Ms. Tate. It seems like we might have a few things we have to deal with. Let me see if I have it straight. You want to know about the performance of your mutual funds, you want confirmation of which mutual funds you have invested in, and you want to know how good your broker is.

Wait for her agreement (she'll likely want to expand on each point — let her); then ask for her permission to ask her some qualifying questions. "Ms. Tate, do you mind if I ask a few questions just to make sure that I understand everything correctly?" When she agrees, begin asking her specific, directed questions on each of the topics. Then, when it comes time to respond, make sure that you respond to each of the things she has brought up:

> Thank you, Ms. Tate. I think as to your first question — how your mutual funds have been doing — your portfolio is now worth $10,285.12. As to your second question — which funds you have in your portfolio — you have the Alpha fund, the Beta fund, and the XYZ fund. None of those fall within our "ethical" fund portfolio, so if you had requested that from your broker it's not what we have here. Actually, if you have an e-mail address or a fax machine, I can send you a list of your port-folio if you'd like. As to the quality of your broker, all I can really tell you is that all of our brokers have gone through rigorous programs and are highly qualified to sell our funds.

When the customer comes back with questions, which she usually will, the questions are more likely to be focused because the way in which you presented the information was focused. Many times the people who come across as unfocused or scatterbrained over the telephone are creative individuals with a strong visual learning style. As much as possible, try to get pictures in front of them — via either fax or e-mail.

Mad at the World

This call can be about something as simple as looking for help in activating a cell phone, but the caller has personal issues and is quite anxious to share them with you. Her husband is useless around the house, her boss gives her an unfair workload, her coworkers are stabbing her in the back, her children don't listen to her. With this customer, short of saying "I'm sorry, ma'am, you have the wrong number — the psychology hotline is 555-1111," there's not much else you can do other than listen. Unless the caller becomes a Time Vampire (see below), you're best off just listening and trying not to encourage her. Whatever you do, avoid commenting on any of her personal opinions and issues. Doing so would risk pushing one of her hot buttons, which could inadvertently direct some of her anger at the world toward you.

Time Vampires

Occasionally, you encounter a customer who just likes to talk. And talk and talk. She's not unpleasant, but she does take up huge amounts of your time. These are typically people who just don't want to, or don't know how to, end a conversation. Either they don't recognize the subtleties of ending a conversation, or they recognize them but don't want to stop the conversation quite yet.

Conversation endings are usually flagged by tone of voice and a verbal signing off. It's an interesting phenomenon, actually. Rather than just say to someone "Okay, I'm going to hang up now," we drop little clues to let the other person know we're ready to get off the phone. Here are some examples.

- Well, John, it's been wonderful speaking with you! Say hi to Gail and the kids for me. . . .
- Okay, then, I'll make sure I have that to you by five o'clock. Just let me know if there is anything else you need. . . .
- Perfect! I'll talk with you again soon. . . .

The Time Vampire either misses or ignores these little clues. With such a caller, the conversations go more like this:

| **You:** | Well, John, it's been wonderful speaking with you! Say hi to Gail and the kids for me. . . . |
| **Vampire:** | Will do. You haven't gotten around to getting married yet, have you? |

| **You:** | Okay, then, I'll make sure I have that to you by five o'clock. Just let me know if there is anything else you need. . . . |
| **Vampire:** | That's great. What are your plans for the weekend? |

| **You:** | Perfect! I'll talk with you again soon. . . . |
| **Vampire:** | Sounds great. How's business, by the way? |

In each of these examples, what the Time Vampire has done is re-open the conversation by asking a question. You find yourself getting sucked back into the conversation and have to work your way back to dropping another clue suggesting that you want to end it. The best technique for overcoming the Time Vampire's re-opening strategy is this: when the Time Vampire continues the conversation with a question, answer it as briefly as possible — in one or two words if you can. Then, without giving her an opportunity to respond to your answer, quickly end the conversation.

| **You:** | Well, John, it's been wonderful speaking with you! Say hi to Gail and the kids for me. . . . |

Vampire:	Will do. You haven't gotten around to getting married yet, have you?
You:	No, not yet! Anyway, take care!

You:	Okay, then, I'll make sure I have that to you by five o'clock. Just let me know if there is anything else you need. . . .
Vampire:	That's great. What are your plans for the weekend?
You:	Same old thing. Call you at five!

You:	Perfect! I'll talk with you again soon. . . .
Vampire:	Sounds great. How's business, by the way?
You:	Couldn't be better! Talk to you soon!

The more persistent Time Vampires might try this re-opening technique a couple of times in a row. Often they are lonely and just looking for a friendly voice to talk to. But although they may have poor social skills, don't confuse this inadequacy with insensitivity. Most would be devastated if they realized how annoying they really are, so be gentle.

The Screamer

Every now and then you find yourself with a caller who is completely out of control and screaming at the top of her lungs. One of her hot buttons has been pushed, she is in full swing, and it seems as though nothing will calm her down. I've heard some rants that have bordered on being completely incomprehensible. While this caller might be one of those who fall into the "it's time to hang up" category (see the end of this chapter), it's equally possible that she is just intensely frustrated.

To begin with, I should identify the one strategy that is guaranteed *not* to work, and that is to tell the caller to "Calm down." Actually, as a general piece of advice, if you ever want to deliberately make somebody more upset than she already is, try telling her to calm down. People don't like being told to calm down, even when they know they need to calm down. Equally unproductive strategies are saying "Please stop screaming" or threatening to hang up.

Generally speaking, the screaming customer doesn't need to be scolded. She needs to be reassured that you care about her, that you want to help her, and that you are able to help her. Your best bet with the screaming caller involves four things.

1. Don't Interrupt

We've talked about listening skills several times throughout the book. Nowhere is careful listening more important than when dealing with the screaming Caller from Hell. Make sure that you let the caller complete her rant until it appears as though she is waiting for a response. I can pretty much guarantee that, if you don't wait and choose to interrupt her, things will only get much worse.

2. Be Willing to Help

Frequently reinforce the message that you really do want to help. When you preface your statements to your caller with that message, you'll find that you get a much better response. So, for example, you could say "Ms. Cooper, I really do want to help you out, but I'm having a hard time understanding you. If I can ask you to speak just a little slower, I'll be able to do a better job for you." This statement sends the clear message that you care.

3. Maintain a Neutral Tone of Voice

In this caller's heightened emotional state, it would be very easy indeed for her to take what you say the wrong way. So a neutral tone of voice is imperative.

4. Confirm Your Understanding

Make sure, before you actually try to resolve the issue, that you truly understand it. It's equally essential that your caller knows that fully understanding the problem is important to you. You need to acknowledge your awareness that she has had a bad experience. Say something like "Ms. Green, it's pretty clear that you have had a very unpleasant experience, and I want to make sure that I completely understand everything. So please jump in if I get any of this wrong." Then repeat to her your understanding of the situation.

Sometimes, of course, there is nothing you can do about the situation. The customer is still not going to get her credit approved, she's still not going to get her refund, and she's still not going to get her part delivered any faster. But with a little effort, hopefully you can bring her emotional state to where you end the call on a more pleasant note than it began.

Not Listening

We've spent a great deal of time in this book talking about improving our listening skills, but what about our callers' listening skills? If you've worked with callers for any length of time, chances are you've encountered at least one customer who appears to be unable or unwilling to listen to anything you have to say. The information goes from one ear to the other without even slowing down in the middle. These types of customers can be completely frustrating when you're in a customer service or technical support function and need to guide a caller through a number of steps.

The best way to deal with the customer who is

"listening-challenged" is to dole out information in very small bursts and then confirm his understanding each step of the way. Whatever you do, don't give him two pieces of information at once — he won't retain them.

Sometimes the person isn't listening because his brain is already ahead of you. He thinks he knows where you're going and leaps ahead, ignoring the details. If this is the case, then the best way to keep your caller grounded to what you're talking about is to pause frequently to confirm his understanding. Make sure you present it properly (i.e., don't say "Do you understand?" in a condescending tone), and make specific reference to one of the elements you were speaking about. For example, "So that's one tablespoon every two hours. . . . Do you have a tablespoon? Good. Now when was the last time you took the medicine? An hour and a half ago? So that means you will take your next tablespoon again at 2:30."

Physical Threats

"You know what?" the caller's deep voice rumbled over the telephone. "If I ever get hold of you, I'm going to beat you to a quivering pulp."

The 50ish-grandmother-of-two collections clerk froze and looked at me in panic. I was monitoring the calls in that company's call center and just happened to be sitting next to her when the call came in. Before I could say anything, she frantically hit the disconnect button. Her face sheet white, she rose without a word and disappeared into the ladies' room. Ten minutes later she returned, and it was obvious she'd been crying. It's amazing how much impact a threat can have — even over the phone. This particular instance was with a caller who didn't know the CSR's name and had no way of knowing that the call center was over 1,000 miles away. Yet the CSR was as frightened as if he were sitting right beside her.

Physical threats are illegal in most countries, and there is only one appropriate way to deal with them. Report the caller to your supervisor, and make sure that he or she, in turn, reports the caller to the police. Unless it's a situation you bring on yourself — perhaps by relentlessly and intentionally pushing the caller's buttons and *trying* to get him upset — there is no justification for physical threats. We'll discuss this more in the "it's time to hang up" section below.

The Liar

I'm always astounded at how easily and shamelessly some people can bring themselves to lie about pretty much anything. It's almost as if no one ever told them that lying was wrong. Even more surprising to me is that, when they get caught, they have no sense of remorse at all. I don't know — maybe they've all just become jaded watching too many politicians at election time. The question is what do you do about them?

I remember sitting next to a CSR for a large on-line retailer. A customer called looking for some special pricing on a product. "Listen," the customer began, "I was talking with someone yesterday, and she told me I could have this for $25!" As the customer was talking, the CSR was showing me on the screen the place where the last CSR who had dealt with this man had typed, in bold letters, "Do not give this guy a deal! I've already explained that he can't have one!"

The CSR gave me kind of a "here we go again" smile and said, "I'm really sorry, sir, there is nothing indicating that on your file, and I'm certainly not authorized to give you that price. I can, however, sell it to you for $50."

The caller became furious and started ranting about the runaround he was getting and how people kept promising him things and not delivering. When he realized the CSR wasn't going to play the game and give in, he finally just said, coolly, "Fine," and hung up.

It's really unfortunate that we have to deal with people like this, and it's not a lot of fun. Actually, the CSR in the above example handled it quite well. Let's go over the principles for dealing with the Liar.

First of all, it's important to recognize that most dishonest people don't think of themselves as being dishonest. Most of them think of themselves as being shrewd or just good at "playing the game." It's not like television, where the evil people actually think of themselves as evil. Coming right out and calling someone a liar, cheat, or thief, therefore, can genuinely offend that person because he doesn't see himself that way. With such customers, you don't have to be unpleasant; you simply have to be firm.

Dealing with the Liar is one of the few cases where you aren't seeking a "win-win" solution, because your customer isn't. The Liar cares only whether or not he wins. Simply stand your ground and try not to say anything that is accusatory or inflammatory.

Incomplete Sentences

Some people . . . well . . . you know . . . they often start a sentence, and . . . it can sometimes be a little . . .

They're not doing it to drive you crazy. Sometimes it's just several thoughts simultaneously colliding in their minds. Sometimes, in their minds, the end of the sentence is so self-evident that it doesn't need to be said. Sometimes they've actually finished the sentence in their heads without realizing that they haven't verbalized the thought. The danger in dealing with people who drop the ends of their sentences is that you become tempted to silently fill in the blanks for them, which can lead to tremendous misunderstandings.

For example, look at this incomplete sentence and see if you can guess what the ending should be: "Given that I'm already paying a hefty price for this one thing . . ."

A.   . . . I'd think you'd throw the other one in for free.

B.   . . . I'm assuming this other piece would cost me a lot as well.

C.   . . . I'll probably have to wait to see if I can afford the other one.

Which is the right answer? Well, how can you know? It's very important, particularly when you're dealing with a challenging situation, that you have all the right information. Don't be afraid to ask questions. Find out exactly what it is that your caller meant.

Chicken Licken (the Sky Is Falling)

It was about half an hour before my seminar was to begin. There were to be 50 people in attendance, and my client was concerned that the hotel hadn't put out enough refreshments. He picked up the phone in the room and called the banquets manager. "We have a huge problem! I have 80 people coming to this event that are going to be here in half an hour, and I promised them that there would be plenty of food to go around. There is not nearly enough here, and I am going to be getting some very grouchy participants! These people have paid good money to get here, and, if they think I'm being chintzy on the refreshments, they are going to be asking for their money back, and I can't afford to be giving all those refunds. You'd better get somebody up here right away and make sure that there is lots of food and lots of drink — cold and hot. I'm going to need at least three times the amount of food you have here! This is going to be a disaster!"

When he hung up the phone, I asked him, "Why the rant? Why didn't you call and just ask for more food?"

My client gave me a blank look. "Isn't that what I just did?" he asked in confusion.

Some people seem to be happiest when they are living their lives in panic mode. And they expend a great deal of effort trying to get others in panic mode too. These people are most notable for their tendency to blow things way out of proportion. When they have to resolve issues, they don't have a problem, they have a *Problem*, and the consequences of their *Problem* not being resolved are dire. Each *Problem* is life or death — the single most important issue they have ever had to face.

With Chicken Licken, you have to walk a fine line between not getting caught up in her hysteria and downplaying her concern so much that she thinks you're not taking her seriously. Your best strategy is to be careful with your tone of voice and to practice your prompting and echoing skills. "Really?" "Is that right?" "Your shipment has to be there by noon tomorrow or you lose your job?" There's really not much else you can do. You could make your tone of voice more frantic to try to convince her that you, too, are taking this matter Very Seriously, but you're really best off projecting confidence, competence, and compassion. The important thing is that Chicken Licken believes she has conveyed to you the importance of her *Problem* and that she is confident you'll be able to help her.

Time to Hang Up

I'm often asked "When is it appropriate to hang up on a caller?" "How much abuse should I be expected to take?" It's a tough question. It has an even tougher answer, though, because it's likely not what you want to hear.

Most arguments for hanging up on a customer hinge on a point where our callers have gone too far. There's a line that they shouldn't cross. We are people, after all, and we deserve to be treated with a certain amount of dignity. Moreover, few of us get paid well enough to put up with that kind of abuse. I agree with all of that.

The difficulty I have with giving people permission to hang up goes back to something we discussed at the beginning of the book — that the vast majority of confrontations we find ourselves in have been caused by *us*. And in most of those cases, like the CSRs who turn to me with baffled looks, unsure why their callers are behaving strangely, we are unaware of our culpability in the conflict. So the question becomes, if there is a chance that you created the confrontation in the first place, if the Caller from Hell is a creature of your own making, do you still have the right to hang up on him or her?

The short answer is yes, there are times when it is appropriate to hang up on your callers. But those times aren't as frequent as you might think. Physical threats? Absolutely. Someone is obviously intoxicated? Yes. Sexual harassment or blatant racism? Of course. But for all the other situations, you really want to think two, three, four times before you cut someone off. Giving up is no substitute for being skilled.

THIS IS YOUR WAKE-UP CALL

Not causeless is this journey to the abyss.
— Dante's *Inferno*

While there are times I'm convinced that the static we hear on the line is actually the sound of Alexander Graham Bell spinning in his grave, I think that, ultimately, he'd be proud of us. We have harnessed his invention in ways that he couldn't have possibly imagined. And the hits just keep coming. Although most of us take these things for granted now, features such as voice mail, caller ID, programmable ring tones, and the like are pretty recent additions to the telephone's repertoire. We are just now dipping our little toes into video telephony, voice-over-IP, and a whole host of new and exciting things. Where the telephone will be in 20 years is anyone's guess, but I have no doubt it will be exciting.

The one thing that won't change, however, the one constant throughout, is people. Regardless of the mode of communication we adopt, regardless of the technology we use, the one wildcard will always be people. And no matter how proficient you become at dialing numbers, you can never be truly effective until you learn how to dial into your callers. The Five Cs of Influence — comprehension, compassion, confidence, competence, and cheerfulness — are more than just guidelines for dealing with people on the phone; they represent the essence of connecting with everyone you encounter.

While you may think of yourself as spending a large proportion of your life on the telephone, I prefer to think of it as spending a large proportion of your life with other people. Living, breathing human beings like you and me, with hot buttons, cold buttons, and a complex set of expectations created by their needs, circumstances, situations, predispositions, and personalities. The better you learn to work with these people, the better you'll be at your job, and the more enjoyment you'll have at work. To learn about people, you have to *like* people. You have to *want* to help them, *want* to listen to them. You have to *care* about them and their problems.

Mr. Bell didn't give us a communication tool. He gave us an opportunity. An opportunity to make a difference in the lives of other people every day. And every time the telephone rings it's up to us to rise to the occasion and answer his call. Have fun!